The Genius Act

The Genius Act: The 99th Percentile Tax Reform & Job Creation Act of 2013.

Introduction

Originally written as potential legislative Act, *The Genius Act*, provides a loose guideline to redeem America's economy to model of excellence status that it has maintained throughout most of its history.

The purpose of the Act shall be as follows:

- To broaden the Treasury's tax base by reforming the tax code to allow for the easing of the tax burden for all who are engaged in new and emerging job classes designated under this Act. It will lower the income tax burden for corporations and individuals covered under *The Genius Act*. *The Genius Act* will also introduce new consumption taxes that will pay for the reduction in taxes that it aims to achieve. Lastly, it aims to lower government obligations and outlays to ensure a prosperous future.

These job classes covered under *The Genius Act* include:

- Military personnel to include all new volunteers in intelligence, linguistics, and all air combat controllers.
- Education personnel including all new teachers and professors in the fields of science, math, and medicine. Visiting professors of extraordinary or "genius of field "merit shall be granted special provisions in tax relief.
- Master farmers and agriculturists who can provide "genius" knowledge to increase the nation's "Growth Food" output.
- New energy development personnel including new energy technology development in fossil and traditional fuel methods.
- A newly created job class of certified tax consultants to be regulated by the Department of the Treasury.
- Law enforcement personnel including all personnel created by the Alcohol, Tobacco, and Firearms (ATF) Authorization Act created by the Genius Act.
- Infrastructure workers at federal and state levels and port workers, merchant marines, and longshoremen.
- Manufacturers who repatriate jobs back into the United States and whose products are at 80% made and assembled in America.

- Employees of the Genius Security Administration who will be responsible for implementing a new social service sector that will eventually replace the Social Security Administration and other government entities.

All jobs created and funded by this Act will be subject to a new progressive tax rate schedule that will spur exponential growth in all sectors as well as support and auxiliary businesses that will be created. Coupled with a higher minimum wage and higher wages earned by those who are currently hidden in the "shadow economy" becoming fully engaged taxpayers this Act would become the model for debt and deficit elimination not just reduction.

The Genius Act morphed into a concept for a Utopian capitalistic society for an increasingly social 21st Century America. Like our ancestors who set off on voyages to discover the "New World" *The Genius Act* aims to pay that opportunity forward equally and create a true Genius Society.

Look What We Would Create!

- 1 Million New Corporations
- 33 Million New Jobs
- $33 Trillion of New Wealth in the Worldwide Economy
- $1 Trillion of new government spending over the 10 year life of the program
- $9-13 Trillion in New Tax Revenue

The federal government will also have the option to apply these new progressive tax rates to all jobs created in all classes for a specified period of time in order to provide incentives for job growth. The recommended period of time for this extension of benefits would be limited to two calendar years. The recommended time period for "Genius" class jobs tax favored status would be no less than 5 years. Along with the creation of the Genius Security Administration to reduce the federal government's future obligations by 50% or more we can eliminate the possibility of any fiscal, monetary, or economic crisis in the future.

The Genius Act© Tax Reforms

The Genius Act will create a new simplified tax rate schedule for all jobs created or funded by the Act. Employees of corporations created by the Genius Act would be granted to exclusive tax favored status under the following revolutionary programs:

The Genius Act

- Creation of the Medical & Retirement Savings Tax to replace Social Security & Medicare payroll taxes for employees and employers. Work income would be reported on newly created W-2GE
- Creation of a Genius Tax Rate Schedule for all income received by "Genius" status taxpayers including retirement plans, capital gains, dividend and interest income. Income tax rates would be lowered but deductions would be limited to cover budget shortfalls.
- New corporate tax rate schedules for "Genius" class job creators to spur economic activity through increases in hiring and production output
- Creation of new National Retirement Savings Accounts and a modified Retirement Savings Credit for "Genius" status taxpayers.
- Introduction of "Vice Tax" initiatives to produce revenue by decriminalizing behavior that has become a burden on the criminal justice system.

The Genius Act Jobs Creation Bills

The Genius Act shall create provisions for several Jobs creation Bills that will be presented to Congress for funding. Congress would then authorize the creation of a cabinet level position to be called the National Jobs Czar. The Jobs Czar along with a newly created Deputy Secretary of Treasury for Workforce Innovation will oversee implementation of several ground breaking programs.

These revolutionary programs if implemented fully would cure the ills of long term unemployment and provide measures for "negative unemployment" or "full employment plus" in the foreseeable future.

These Jobs Bills would include the following:

- Creation of the first national Water G.R.I.D (Gathering Removal Inland Distribution) system to decrease the harmful effects of hurricanes and super storms on America's coastlines.
- The Prison Reform & Reconciliation Act to create " Genius Wage Jobs for non-violent felons to have working wages while they serve their sentences and obtain skilled trades before their release back into Society.
- The Farm Aid of 2013 would fund the creation of the Master Growth Food Project as well as the Goodwill Farming Project to develop new food sources through the use of alternative energy sources to grow food on federally appointed lands and military bases.
- The Military Reassignment Jobs Act to train veterans and honorably discharged military personnel in newly created job classes of Agricultural Engineers and Energy Engineers.

Combat veterans will be given preference in receiving transition jobs through the Army Core of Engineers.

- The Repatriation of Manufacturing Jobs Bill for multi-national corporations who reinvest in new manufacturing jobs or new products that are more than 80 percent made of American made parts. This would include an Alternative Energy and Hydroponic Growth Provision as a joint venture with the Department of the Interior, Environmental Protection Agency, and the Department of Agriculture to accelerate the use of indoor growth facilities and spur investment in new energy technology.
- Creation of the Certified Tax Preparer program with the Department of the Treasury to subsidize the cost of Income Tax preparation for nearly all taxpayers who use nationally trained tax preparers.
- The Genius Wage Reform Act to raise the minimum wage to at least $9.00 per hour while decreasing payroll tax liabilities or the most vulnerable workers to increase their spending power to perpetually stimulate the economy.

Social Changes to Create a Genius Society!

The Genius Act will pursue a progressive agenda through legislative and social programs that will create the greatest generation in American civilization: The Genius Society. Similar to FDR's New Deal or LBJ's Great Society the *Genius Act* aims to fast forward America on a new path of greatness through the implementation of various initiatives including:

- **Voting Rights Act of 2013-** Legislative act that if implemented would make the first Tuesday of November not the first a National holiday to allow for voting on all federal and state referendum initiatives. The law would also Include a mandate for National same day registration in all states to increase voter turnout.
- **Welfare Reform Act of 2013-** Legislation to allow states to require unemployed recipients of state and federal assistance to be required to perform volunteer service of 20 hours per month and to be recertified bi-annually with exclusions for elderly, disabled, student, and veteran recipients.
- **America Bikes Program-** Wellness program designed to encourage healthy lifestyles by sponsoring an initiative of using celebrities and athletes to promote bike riding for children and adults for daily exercise and offering tax credits to bicycle manufacturers and on bicycle purchases.
- **Food for Guns-** Social program sponsored by the Department of Agriculture to remove assault rifles and other dangerous weapons by offering sustenance assistance cards in return for the weapons being destroyed.

- **Goodwill Farming Program & Farm Corporation of America-** International farming initiative to help developing and emerging nations improve food growing conditions using state of the art growth technology and techniques.
- **Women's Reproductive Rights Act-** Legislation that will allow National Women's Centers (newly created Planned Parenthood and Family Planning Service Centers) to be moved to military bases to ensure availability in all states.
- **Immigration Reform Act of 2013-** New revolutionary immigration plan to bring all immigrants into Genius Society in order to provide better tracking and increased economic impact of newly added workers.

New Industries or Economies of Scale to be created by the Genius Act!

The last vital component of ingenuity presented in the Genius Act will be its effect on business innovation that will result in brand new industries and economies of scale that will pave the way for the new "Industrial Revolution". Key industries and economies to be created include:

- **The National Farmer's Market-** National distribution network to bring fresh meat and produce to America's working class families while using logistics technology from the private sector to increase efficiency.
- **Creation of the first Genius Security Number (GSN)-** a new 13 digit numbering system used to track citizens and resident aliens who live and work under the Genius Act system. This will also include the creation of the Genius Security Services Corporation as a new financial reporting agency for income and retirement services including medical coverage.
- **Federal Business & Health Care Complex-** Federally owned and operated business centers that would be a hub for food sources and health care to ensure equality of resources. Complexes would be added to every military base to maximize their useful life.
- **Water G.R.I.D Project-** Federally funded desalination project to protect America's coastlines and casualty insurance industries by moving sea water inland to create brand new water sources for human and animal consumption.
- **Genius Act Trade Treaty (GATT)-** Trade agreement to be entered into with emerging and developing nations in South America and Africa to use American agricultural technology and food growing techniques to create a new class of wealth both foreign and domestically.
- **Tax Preparer & Health Care Administration Professional-** Pilot program to be created by the Department of the Treasury to subsidize the cost of federal tax preparation for all taxpayers as well as serve to administer the mandate of Affordable Care Act.

The Genius Act

The *Genius Act* will address many controversial issues and propose many revolutionary innovations in order to generate conversation around what can be done to maintain America's elite status perpetually? While balancing empirical and analytical research to prove the effectiveness of its implementation *Genius Act* will focus more on a vast abundance of social research about how to define greatness in a highly informed, rapidly attention shifting society. It will focus on incentivizing innovation in both business and social arenas to reaffirm our place as the "Land of Opportunity". It will discuss in depth all of the principles that made America great: agrarian and manufacturing dominance, business innovation and efficiency, and social awareness and adaptation. It will also work to bring America's shadow economy to the light by giving undercover workers and entrepreneurs an incentive to become fully productive members of the "real" economy.

The *Genius Act* seeks to become the 21st Century's equivalent of the previous century's New Deal or Great Society as the model of Progressive advancement. It also seeks to rival the Industrial Revolution as source for widespread business innovation and economic expansion. However, unlike its predecessors it takes aim at these targets simultaneously and not mutually exclusively. It will also pursue a plan to save millions of working class Americans from financial ruin due to chronic illness and disease allowing them to provide for their families perpetually.

These initiatives will also include a health care revolution to rid the world of the most infectious, chronic, and terminal illnesses by funding research and providing tax incentives to pharmaceutical companies who discover chemical remedies to these diseases. Educational institutions and professional organizations including professional sports franchises will be encouraged to fund and maintain research hospitals that will adapt to the healthcare issues of the future. They will be charged with maintaining a database of medical history results of all treated patients that will enable better tracking of medical trends and reduce costs by allocating resources before illnesses become epidemic. Lastly, there will be an overall charge to create a Women's Wellness Program that will address a full life cycle of female issues and make them priority one of any new health care initiative.

In the aftermath of the Great Recession the *Genius Act* will provide a blueprint for the greatest peaceful economic expansion in American history. In Part 1, we will discuss the Job creation Acts needed to bring America back to "full employment and beyond" while elevating the wealth of the world's emerging and developing nations. In Part 2, we will discuss how to employ those who have long lived in the shadows or the unemployable: illegal immigrants and prisoners and felons. In Part 3, we will discuss tax reforms, the "Genius Tax Rate Schedule" and the "Genius Society" wage scale. In Part 4, we will discuss the social changes and programs needed to bring America to elite "Genius Society" status. Finally in Part 5, we will discuss the business innovation and corporation and economy of scale creation needed to ensure that status perpetually. May God Bless America!

The Genius Act

Table of Contents

The Genius Act

Part 1: The Job Creators

Even in the recovery from The Great Recession in which corporate profits have risen to levels never seen before and witnessed the meteoric rise of the stock market indices to record levels there still remained one problem; sustained high unemployment. In an effort to correct this problem the *Genius Act* aims to address this by presenting various job creation acts that if implemented would solve this problem forever. While not delving into the research of all of the various laws surrounding each of these acts, *Genius Act* wants to present the ideas to spark the discussion before changes are made through the law making process.

I.   The Farm Aid & Master Food Authorization Act

The United States Department of Agriculture (USDA) pursuant to the *Genius Act* will introduce legislation to revamp the current Farm Aid Bill and create the Master Food Program. This Act will provide coordination between the USDA and other federal agencies including: Department of Defense, Veteran's Affairs, Department of Justice, and Department of Homeland Security to secure and grow America's food sources. All jobs created under this Act will be subject to the new Genius Level corporate tax rates (to be detailed later in this book) and all employees would subject to Genius Level income tax rates (also to be explained later). This Act will cover many aspects of the Agricultural Industrial Complex including:

- Alternative Energy Source Growing Methods
- Insourcing food growth projects on federal lands including military bases and Federal Correctional Institutes.
- Creating a distribution network through a National Farmer's and Butcher's Market to subsidize food costs to working class families.
- Streamline food programs to increase efficiency and eliminate waste.
- To create an unlimited supply and demand for agricultural workers earning a living wage through the creation of several revolutionary programs.

Most of the programs would be social programs but would also create jobs for workers who have previously left the workforce including:

- Debt to Society Farming Corporation
- Work for Food Stamps Program
- Volunteer to Workforce Program
- Genius Wage Program for Immigrant Farm Workers
- Guns for Food Program
- Creation of the Farm Corp Volunteer Program & Goodwill Farm Project.
- Master Growth Food Project

The Genius Act

Throughout America's history the key to our success as a society was our dedication to agricultural and manufacturing dominance, however as we became reliant on innovation of industrial processes and moved to a more service based economy we lost the value and importance of "Made in America" as our symbol of excellence. *Genius Act* aims to become the source document for a new millennium of economic prosperity for America and its trade partners by reemphasizing our agricultural and manufacturing dominance while taking full advantage of technological advances. In addition we will encourage the Department of Commerce to develop a Genius Act Trade Treaty (GATT) to form more mutually beneficial economic partnerships with our allies and adversaries a like to ensure a peaceful prosperity paradigm for the foreseeable future.

Alternative Energy Source Priority

The purpose for this project is to develop sustainable food production without the use of fossil fuels for power. The Master Growth Food Project shall utilize solar, wind, and hydroponic energy and growing techniques in order to maintain future food production. The Project will develop sustainability and development plans to create growth environments even in the most extreme conditions. Sustainability reports will be archived by the USDA in order to facilitate development of new projects with comparable conditions. The USDA will also develop a training program to develop a public-private partnership with enterprising entrepreneurs who will further these technologies. We will encourage the development of worldwide economies of scale by offering tax favored status to enterprises that can help achieve and maintain this objective. Credits will also be given to enterprises that can develop new biomass fuel sources with foreign trade partners under provisions of the Genius Act Trade Treaty (GATT). The United States will pursue a trade agreement with China to sell natural gas at a discount spot rate to help them improve energy conservation and air quality measures. This would include infrastructure improvements to increase storage capacity here and in China as well pipeline improvements to include other trade partners.

Insourcing of Agricultural Jobs

The preeminent goal for the Master Food Project is to insource agricultural on federal lands including federal correctional institutes and military bases. The USDA, in conjunction with the Department of Defense and the Department of Justice will employ researchers to develop a feasibility study for each federal property including all FCI's and a vast majority of military bases and duty stations. Individual reports will determine resources needed to make each site energy and food source independent within 3 years. Energy independence projects along with connections to the Water G.R.I.D. will move forward first followed by agricultural projects. Private sector companies will be charged with implementing energy recommendations and constructing growth sites. Training programs will be instituted simultaneously for prisoners and soldiers alike on protocol and essential job duties. Once training is completed food projects will commence with estimate time of deployment not to exceed 2 fiscal years. All non-deployed veterans who expect to de-enlist within two years of the program's deployment will be given first priority in enrollment in the program.

Master Growth Food Project

The cornerstone of the Genius Act Farm Bill would be the creation of the nation's first Master Growth Food Project. The purpose of the project is to use traditional and non-traditional growing techniques and methods to teach prisoners and military personnel both active and retired how to become independent farmers, ranchers, and agriculturalists. They will learn how to maintain and harvest foods to be sold at the newly created National Farmer's Market that will provide subsidized goods for citizens to purchase locally at weekend open air markets. They will also learn techniques to grow and manage livestock of poultry, beef, and pork to be sold at local meat and dairy markets for profit. The MGFP will also create indoor growth facilities for plants and animals to expand growth cycles for each while using alternative energy methods. These indoor facilities will use solar panels and wind energy to power the facilities and experiment with hydroponic growth methods to improve organic food availability of consumable foods for consumers as well for feeding of livestock to be consumed. Foods grown will be first made available to these facilities so that they may become self-sufficient. Any excess products will then be provided at subsidized rates to state and local prison systems to minimize costs. Any products remaining will be sold at local markets or provided to goodwill efforts to needy families. As these farms grow and produce more excess products it will lead to the formation of the National Farmer's Market and Butcher Store.

As a part of a Military Budget & Reform Act to be detailed later in the *Genius Act*, there would be a provision to reallocate funds from the Department of Defense budget to provide military support and personnel to the Master Growth Food Project. The Army Corp of Engineers will create and train two new job classes under their direction. These new job classes will be called Agricultural Engineer and Energy Engineer.

Agricultural Engineer trainees will engage in training techniques that will allow them to secure and maintain America's food sources including fruit and vegetables, dairy and poultry. They will work alongside civilian management and their own commanding officer administration to provide security to the project. They will be actively involved in the leadership and training of other personnel which will include local and migrant workers and assigned inmates to the Project. Energy engineers will focus on creating energy stability and independence for military installations in general but exclusively for Master Food Projects both foreign and domestically.

The Genius Act

National Farmer's Market & Butcher Store

As output of food produced grows, the Master Food Project will work alongside cooperative farmers to form a domestic distribution network to be called the National Farmer's Market. The USDA will be responsible for locating or developing a local open air marketplace in every metropolitan area with a population of 100,000 or more. Farmers and food wholesalers will sign up for the cooperative farmer program in order to purchase produce, poultry, and dairy products at discount rates. Each farmer or wholesaler will receive a Distributor number for accounting purposes and products will be price fixed locally to be competitive with other locally produced products. Products will be eligible for USDA Supplemental Nutrition Assistance Program (SNAP) benefits and co-op farmers will be encouraged to join the program in order to increase sales and receive reimbursements. The Department of Agriculture will also develop programs to take payments mobile. The USDA will also encourage the creation of a Fish & Meat Market to sell these products nationally as they are produced by this project. The model of this program shall be used to establish markets on foreign lands through the Goodwill Food Project.

Agro Business Reform

The Master Food Program Initiative shall have a priority in cutting waste and inefficiency by gradually reducing subsidies to large farming corporations in lieu of making investments in the Co-op Farm Program and the volunteer based Farm Corp to secure the growth of essential foods such as: fruits and vegetables, poultry and dairy products. Large farm corporations shall only receive grants and subsidies once they have established new Genius class organizations that employs and utilizes independent contractors that would be subject to Genius class tax rates or they fund a Master Growth Food Project inside an FCI or military base. They would also have to set up new Food Program Identification Numbers in order to track their impact on individual citizens' nutritional satisfaction. Emphasis will be placed on establishing cooperative farming operations in America's cities to ensure effective distribution of food resources.

This version of The Farm Aid Act would go beyond the reach of the current FARRM Act by adding Genius Act addendums that would restore the United States to its agricultural roots by providing the means to ensure that the economy has an unlimited supply and demand for agricultural workers to feed the world through the following revolutionary programs:

Debt to Society Programs®

As a part of a wide ranging Prison Reform Act the Genius Farm Aid Act would authorize inmates at Federal Corrections Institutes (FCI) to be allowed to enroll in the Master Growth Food Project. These inmates would learn to grow food during their sentences which would allow them to earn a living wage during their sentence as well as support their dependent families.

The Genius Act

Genius Act will encourage the Department of Justice to disband the penal wage system and instead replace it with a wage system that would begin at a level that would start at a minimum of 60% of the Genius wage and allow the inmates pay to rise as they acquire more skills and technical training. They also would be offered transitional jobs in the program complete with housing assistance once they have completed their sentences.

Work for Food Stamps Program

In conjunction with state welfare agencies recipients of SNAP benefits will be required to provide volunteer work hours equal to a minimum of 20 per month if they are not currently employed or continuing their education. Exceptions would be granted for elderly, disabled and veteran recipients. All recipients would have to recertify their qualifications for the program after 180 days and would be given a 30 day grace period to complete the requirements or have their eligibility denied. Preferential assignments will be given to those who choose to work with co-op farmers or those who participate in the National Farmer's Market and would qualify them for additional benefits and fresh food grants at the Farmer's Market. Corporations and restaurants who participate in the Food Program will also be able to receive volunteers to assist in their daily operations would include chain operations. Volunteers who work in chain restaurants would then be able to use their SNAP benefits for cooked food alternatives.

Volunteer to Workforce Program

In conjunction with the agencies of workforce innovation and TANF benefits suppliers, the Genius Act will recommend the creation of a new program to be called Volunteer to Workforce. Recipients of unemployment assistance and/or SNAP benefits will be eligible to work for Genius employers in the food Industry including grocery stores and restaurants. Workers would receive in-kind benefits such as gift certificates and gift cards to the employer they are working for or to partner corporations for products such as gas cards or clothing. Employers would be able to provide volunteers with benefits up to $10 per hour tax free with consideration to hire recipients as full or part time employees once they have volunteered a minimum of 300 hours. Recipients will be able to work up to 1,000 hours per year. Employers will be able to fully deduct any benefits given as charitable contributions and employees would be able to receive the benefits tax free as long as they have no other income sources of than unemployment assistance. The maximum federal tax obligation would be 9% of the benefits received and would become the responsibility of the employer if the recipient is hired to a full time paid position. Companies would be encouraged to utilize workers in their shipping and logistics departments or in customer service entry level positions. The chief recipients of these benefits should be parents of dependent children that are unable to receive support from the non-custodial parent and for chronically unemployed persons.

The Genius Act

Genius Wage Act for Migrant Agricultural Workers

The Master Food Program will extend the invitation to unskilled agricultural workers who are currently undocumented, seeking citizenship or work visas to enter the United States with the expressed opportunity to work with co-op farmers or at Master Food Project sites. Participants in the program will be eligible for Genius level tax rates and retirement status. This program along with the extension of the Deferred Action on Childhood Arrivals (DACA) and the DREAM Act will act as the cornerstones of the Genius Immigration Reform Act to be detailed later. The Genius Wage Act will require that agricultural workers remain employed for 17 of 20 quarters that they are enrolled in the program or complete volunteer work hours at Master Food Projects during unemployment periods. They will be eligible to receive SNAP benefits and fresh food grants from co-op farmers during times of unemployment.

Guns for Food Program®

The USDA along with the Bureau of Alcohol, Tobacco, and Firearms will enact a program that will allow citizens who return guns and assault weapons, with assault weapons receiving a premium designation. Citizens will in return receive a prepaid SNAP benefit card that will allow them to purchase food at retail locations across America through the EBT system. It will also allow them to purchase fresh food through the co-op farmer program. Grants will also be given to retailers who enroll in the program and provide gifts to their customers for returning weapons. State and local agencies will be able to apply for block grants to assist in anonymous tip programs that help remove illegal weapons from cities and felony offenders. The program will call for a $250 benefit for all handguns and a $500 benefit for all assault weapons. A separate benefit of $250 will be provided for high capacity magazine clips that hold 30 or more rounds.

Creation of the Farm Corporation of America (Farm Corp)

In a model of the Peace Corp the USDA will create a volunteer farming program that will be charged with creating Master Food Projects across America and on foreign lands. Volunteers shall enlist in the Corp for a minimum of 3 years in which they will receive energy and agricultural training as well as minimal military training and linguistics training on foreign projects. Participants shall receive a stipend equal to $33,000 per year but with the potential to earn bonuses as they achieve training certifications as well as shareholder bonuses as their projects turn profits or reach production targets. Undocumented resident aliens and local farmers on foreign Master Food Projects will be allowed to use their service time in order to qualify for citizenship status. In addition, as a part of a Genius Military Budget Reduction Act we will explore the possibility of creating Goodwill Master Food Projects in foreign lands to secure food sources for our allied partners, emerging and developing nations and nutritionally distressed territories. The Department of Commerce will work with our trade partners internationally to develop the wide ranging Genius Act Trade Treaty to forge new economic partnerships through food security.

Creation of the National Food Complex

Under the direction of the USDA Genius Act will call for the creation of an open marketplace for fresh and organic foods including poultry, dairy, and seafood to be made available to the general taxpayer on military bases and other federally appropriated lands. Likewise there would be a similar Commissary Complex to be made available to military personnel and their families. Wal-Mart would be targeted along with other large retailers to form public-private partnerships to provide logistical support to these complexes while allowing Wal-Mart to setup their Marketplace Food Centers on military bases and use public lands to build Food Complexes in the inner city.

The ability to feed one's self is the most basic of necessities and while America had accomplished all of the technical ability to feed the entire nation we had begun to take that ability for granted while moving toward a more service based economy. *Genius Act* urges society to create the demand and supply for the workforce to move back to our agrarian and manufacturing roots by incentivizing innovation, integration, infrastructure and implementation of ideas that garner a new generation of growth. By reviving America's metropolitan areas we can use our infrastructure superiority to keep up with the pace of business.

The Goodwill Food & Energy Project

The Department of Defense along with the Departments of Agriculture and Interior will develop a partnership with allied foreign governments where we currently have military operations or consulates. This project will also encourage development of projects near the world's refugee and temporary housing camps in order to encourage peace and prosperity. The United States would agree to remove military personnel in favor of building sustainable food and energy sources at these locations. National Farmer's Market participants will be given first priority bidding on distribution projects to provide food and energy sources until official Goodwill Projects can be established. Indigenous fruits and vegetable will be grown in order to develop an export market with other nations that will be covered under the Genius Act Trade Treaty.

II.   **The Repatriation of Manufacturing Jobs Bill**

The Genius Act will include a provision to fund tax reform measures that would bring Genius tax rates to corporations that employ Americans in manufacturing jobs. These measures would also incorporate Genius Tax zones for regions of the country that have experienced the largest loss of economic activity. These tax rates would apply to all of their employees and these corporations will also be able to receive tax relief on profits that they repatriate from their parent multinational corporations. Special tax provisions will be given to individuals and corporations who purchase equipment from the following manufacturing classes:

- Solar, wind, and alternative energy equipment
- Bicycle and high efficiency motorcycles
- High efficiency farm equipment
- Heating and cooling systems
- Electrical equipment and Water GRID materials makers
- Manufacturers of vehicles with an average fuel economy of 40 miles per gallon
- Makers of fuel efficient High Occupancy Vehicles including ship & Ferry makers, train and subway system manufacturers, and aeronautical manufacturers.

Tax favored status covered under Genius tax rate schedule will apply to the manufacturers and to all of the companies in their supply chain. Manufacturers will be eligible to receive tax favored status if their products are at least 80 percent built and assembled inside the continental United States or with special provisions made for products made in Canada or Mexico through the NAFTA law. The Genius Act Trade Treaty (GATT) will encourage these countries to allow tax favored status to its citizens and corporations who supply these manufacturers. Genius level tax rates would apply to manufacturers and their suppliers who apply for Genius class distinction. Genius class rates would apply to Royalty Income that manufacturers and suppliers pay to use patents, copyrights, and trademarks for newly created products. Corporations will also be subject to Genius level tax rates on sales made to foreign governments who the United States establishes Genius Act Trade Treaties with.

GATT 2013: Genius Act Trade Treaty of 2013

The United States will foster trade agreements with under developed and emerging nations to foster food production growth and alternative energy development. These nations will have access to state of the art technology and equipment to reduce costs in building infrastructure. They will be encouraged to build and improve ports and transportation systems including rail systems and interconnecting highways. The United States will sponsor the establishment of Master Food Projects with the backing of local farmers and military personnel to secure these resources long term. The preferred nations to set GATT treaties would include: Brazil, Paraguay, Argentina, Spain, Italy, Ireland, Kenya, Panama, Uruguay, and Belize. Foreign Master Growth Food Projects will be created in all Caribbean and South American nations. Migrant workers from these nations will be given first right of refusal to United States citizenship status if qualified under the Genius Immigration Reform Act to be detailed later. There will also be guest worker program that will allow producers of textiles and other manufactured goods to join the

The Genius Act

Genius Society and receive Genius wages while helping American textile companies return to dominance.

Genius Act Business Redevelopment Zones

In order to foster an environment of economic prosperity the Genius Act will encourage the Department of Commerce and the Department of Treasury to craft economic "war zone" maps that consist of crime ridden, high unemployment or under employment, high emigration areas that will be ground zero as a real life economic experiment of low tax, high consumption, high immigration economic melting pot not seen since the American Industrial Revolution. These zones will be concentrated on states that have the highest long-term unemployment rates which would include:

Florida, Nevada, Michigan, New Jersey, New Mexico, Arizona, and Ohio

Cities with high rates of violent and property crimes:

Detroit MI, St. Louis, Mo, Chicago, IL, Memphis, TN, Gary, IN, Fresno and Oakland, CA

Cities with high levels of emigration and under employment:

Flint, MI, Akron, OH, Milwaukee, WI, Pittsburg, PA, Little Rock, AR, Hartford, CT, Newark, NJ.

The Genius Act will encourage the US government to grant Genius level tax rates to all new employees and Genius corporate tax rates to all new enterprises created in these states and selected metropolitan areas to spur economic growth and to bring America back to full employment status. Along with the Genius Act Infrastructure Jobs which will accelerate consumption and lower transportation costs this Manufacturing Jobs Bill aims to usher in a new Manufacturing Gilded Age based on technological innovation and the desire for energy independence. Along with public-private partnerships to sponsor the infrastructure needs the Genius Act aims to ensure that stimulus spending has its optimum effect by getting the money in the hands of the individuals and entities that need it the most. Lastly, by creating jobs that prevent catastrophe and maintenance our aging infrastructure system we can reduce our reliance on consumption as our source for creating wealth. Redevelopment zones will also offer experimental "vice" zones to allow decriminalization of certain activities with enforced taxes on these activities in order to boost tax revenue in some of America's most crippled economies. "Vice Tax" revenue would be split evenly between the federal and state law enforcement agencies in an enhanced effort to maintain order. Redevelopment areas should be limited to a 4 miles squared radius to increase community involvement. There would also be an increase of factory and manufacturing activity to attract the world's most productive workers to provide a new perspective of the work ethic that made America great.

The Genius Act

Immigration Initiative

As a part of a larger immigration reform act, *The Genius Act* proposes that government agencies encourage incoming immigrants settle in these redevelopment zones with credits being given to corporations and entities that provide sponsorship to new employees. These employees would be required to register under the Genius Security Administration and be subject to mandatory identity verification and income reporting. Government entities in these redevelopment zone areas will be encouraged to recruit immigrants who possess degrees in engineering, science, and technology including those with strong manufacturing backgrounds to make their home in these areas. All new residents who register for the Genius ID program will also have the incentive of lower federal income tax liabilities as well as an expedited path to citizenship after meeting compliance guidelines. Their children who reach the age of 18 and meet other Genius Act Immigration guidelines would automatically be granted US citizenship along with Genius Tax favored status. Urban housing developers in these zones will be eligible for loans that will be equivalent to the federal funds rate to build and maintain commercial and residential properties in the redevelopment zone. Preference in Genius applications will be given to current citizens of BRIC (Brazil, Russia, India, and China) nations so that the US may foster economic relations with these nations with special emphasis on energy efficiency technologies and improvement of air quality worldwide. Genius residents may apply for residency status for their immediate family members and primary care giver after one year of satisfactory residency.

Genius Textile Factory Worker Program

As a part of the Manufacturing Jobs Bill and the American Dream Immigration Reform Act special provisions will be made for textile workers from developing and emerging nations such as: India, Malaysia, Thailand, Cambodia, Taiwan, China, The Philippines, and Singapore; to join the Genius Society and become workers in American factories making Genius wages to produce textiles and other manufactured goods. The factories would be built in Genius Business Redevelopment Zones while Commerce officials negotiate to build comparable factories in each of these nations that would equal American factory conditions with Genius class wages promised in future foreign factories. Workers would undergo language immersion training and would be encouraged to come over with their nuclear families while entering the program. Corporations who build factories in Genius Business Redevelopment Zones will receive tax credits equal to 10% of their building and amortization costs up to $10 million per year for the next 5 years. Up to 100,000 workers per year will be allowed to enter the United States for the next 5 years. All corporations who build factories or employ textile workers will be subject to Genius corporate income tax rates and workers will be eligible for Medical & Retirement Savings benefits.

The Genius Act

III.   The Infrastructure Fund & Water G.R.I.D Creation Act

The Genius Act will provide a plan to provide funding to create the first Infrastructure & Logistics Bank. This will become a full service investment bank which will provide interest free or low interest loans to government entities on all levels to improve infrastructure conditions across the nation. These projects shall include:

- Road improvements and maintenance including connecting at least 1 million more miles to the interstate system to diversify corporation domiciling.
- Railroad Improvement and Construction to improve total miles covered and serviced by the national rail service including transcontinental railroad systems in North and South America. This will be the second component of the Million Miles Program as the program will aim to create 1 Million more miles of newly constructed rail systems inside developing cities across America. The third leg of the Million More Miles program will be employed on the continent of Africa to help develop rail and road systems on that continent.
- Pier & Port improvements and Upgrades including dredging projects at expanding ports.
- Electric GRID improvements and upgrades including alternative energy source improvements.
- Creation of the first national Water GRID system and desalination project
- Pipeline improvements and approval new pipeline projects like the Keystone Pipeline XL to increase capacity of current pipelines and storage capacity. To increase water and fuel line capacity by 1 million miles each to protect coastlines and water supplies.

Issuance of interest free loans will be made through a Trustee Review Board who will serve as management and administration of the Infrastructure & Logistics Bank (ILB). Loans will be guaranteed by the US Treasury and the regional Federal Reserve banks. Shares of the ILB shall be offered to institutional investors to purchase in advance of its inception. Shareholders will receive Genius tax status on any dividend or interest payments received from the ILB. Ownership shares will remain static for a period of no less than 3 years at which the Bank's board may authorize an Initial Public Offering to increase private capital funding. The Board of directors and senior management will be under the authority of the Secretary of Transportations and a newly elected Assistant Secretary of Treasury.

All entities will be encouraged to create limited liability corporations along with a newly created Genius Identification Number (GIN) to handle funds received from the Bank and to manage new employees who will be subject to new Genius level income tax rates. These newly formed entities will be encouraged to make loans to local corporations who will meet the criteria of employing Genius class employees. Any profits or net interest payments received will be subject to Genius corporate tax rates. All employees will be eligible for Genius level tax rates as well as enrollment in the Medical & Retirement Savings Act.

The newly created entities will make private-public partnership loans to infrastructure companies at prime rates for companies that will compete for contracts to complete construction and improvement work. The companies that will qualify for these loans will include:

- Trucking and transportation services including tractor and trailer manufacturers as well as their parts suppliers.
- Port workers and longshoremen and stevedores as well as merchant marines and their unions.
- Makers of sea going merchant vessels including provisions for interest free loans for vessels that use alternative fuel sources including solar, natural gas, or biofuel combustible engines. This will also include makers of shipping containers so that they may upgrade their fleets through the newly created Cash for Containers® program that will offer tax credits of up to $5000 per container that is more than 10 years old that is destroyed and recycled.
- Logistics companies and trade authorities including quasi government entities who regulate transportation and trade.

All jobs and corporations created will be subject to Genius level tax rates and eligible for Medical & Retirement Savings Act benefits. Veterans will be given preference and tax credit bonuses for filling these jobs.

Million More Miles Project®

As a part of the Genius Act a new infrastructure development project shall be created to dramatically increase the presence of interstate highway coverage and workable railway coverage. The program will be named the Million More Miles program with its goal lying within the name. The program aims to increase or replace 1 million miles interstate highways with an emphasis on developing routes that would allow efficient travel from America's Midwestern manufacturing hubs like St. Louis, Detroit, Chicago, and Indianapolis through the oil boom Great Plains to west coast. There also would be emphasis on developing routes to the Atlantic and Gulf port regions. The development of these new and replacement highways shall take place over a 10 year period with an annual report due to Congress to track improvements.

The Genius Act

This program would also be implemented in relation to the nation's railroad and rail transit systems in America's large and emerging cities. The emphasis will be to improve the metro rail systems in big cities while developing or enhancing rail services in all of America's emerging metropolitan areas especially those in the South and Atlantic seaboard. Along with developing urban-suburban metro rail systems there will also be an emphasis on developing and improving rail systems between manufacturing and warehouse districts and these cities port districts. These projects along with the Million More Miles Water & Fuel Pipeline Projects would dramatically improve the nation's infrastructure of water systems and fuel transportation. Eventually these programs would be expanded through the Genius Act Trade Treaty to include expansion into foreign infrastructure improvements.

Water G.R.I.D Creation Act

In conjunction with the Department of the Interior and the Army Corp of Engineers, *The Genius Act* proposes that the United States shall fund and maintain the first of its kind Gathering Removal Inland Distribution (GRID) system to trace the coastline of the Gulf and Atlantic coasts. The system shall be composed of a vacuum piping system that would periodically move water from the seas to locations inland where water sources are desperately needed. After transportation from coastline areas water shall be treated, filtered, and desalinated for distribution to irrigation systems used in conjunction with Master Growth Food Projects.

 The Genius Act also proposes that as a part of the Million Miles Pipeline Project the water be dispersed throughout the Southwestern and western United States to alleviate drought and water shortage conditions. As a matter of national defense and border security there shall be a "Grande" pipeline to run directly through the United States-Mexico border that will contain pipelines for water and natural gas to increase storage capacity at western ports.

The Department of the Army shall be the lead agency in developing the technology to create the Water GRID. The Army would develop a job class that will be charged with building the GRID with military and civilian personnel working side by side. Army personnel will work along with civilian welding and plumbing engineers to connect the GRID to city and rural water systems in order to replenish ground water shortages in drought prone and low water areas. This water shall also be moved to areas on federal lands such as military bases and FCI to provide water sources for the newly formed Master Growth Food Project areas. These projects will provide systems to desalinate the water and filter it can be basin water sources for hydroponic food growth under solar and wind energy sources.

The GRID shall be used to remove water from coastline and inland water areas in advance of an approaching hurricane or super storm. The GRID will employee up to 30,000 military and civilian personnel in the building of the GRID system and 5,000 maintenance personnel during the next 5 fiscal years. Preference in job placement in civilian positions to discharged veterans. The Water GRID shall be funded and maintained using a special carry interest charge on every flood insurance policy written throughout the life of the program. A surplus fund shall be created based on profits from the Master Growth Food Project.

The special carry interest charge shall be called the GRID surcharge will be equivalent to 1% of all flood insurance policies written in Atlantic and Gulf coast states. Insurance and re-insurance agencies shall maintain a non-interest bearing escrow account to be paid to the Water GRID Insurance Administration.

The Master Growth Food Project shall pay a surcharge to the administration for each gallon used in growth projects. Excess water shall be moved to high drought areas for the creation of a MIST system to hydrate low water areas during high temperature times. The GRID system will also be connected to inner city sewer systems to allow the water supplies to be replenished and flush impurities.

The Army Corp of Engineers will also have the authority along with the Department of the Interior to create a border defense and energy system that will encompass the nautical area between 12 and 20 miles away from the coastline. This area shall include wind energy production equipment as well as a dam system that would funnel water to the GRID system. This would also provide a defense checkpoint system for the US Coast Guard to patrol the coastline. Here is a preview of the economic impact that would be produced if the Water GRID was created:

Job Creation and Revenue Estimates for creation of Water GRID				
Jobs Created	Average Salary	Average Retirement Contribution %	Average Federal Income Tax Liability %	Medical Savings Contribution %
Direct Employment Jobs (100,000)	42,400	6.8	16.8	4.5
Indirect/Support Systems (26,000-35,000	54,800	5.5	15.9	4.5

Estimate of annual revenue if, 1% Water Grid surcharge is applied to 100 million coastal homes and residences with average policy of $900 per residence is **$900 million.**

Revenue generated from water usage tax on all water displaced from coastal areas to inland sources at $ .10/gallon if 100 billion gallons used is **$10 billion**

Average annual savings on flood insurance loss claims is **$3.2 billion** or more depending on flood events per year.

Here is an estimate of the jobs and average salaries' of those jobs that would be created if the Infrastructure Bill was fully implemented.

Jobs Creation Estimate for Infrastructure Fund (Job Class)	Jobs Created in this Class	Average Income for Jobs Created
Road Improvements	25,000-30,000	$62,000
Railroad Improvements & Construction	5,000-10,000	$53,000
Port & Pier Improvements	45,000-60,000	$48,000
Electric GRID Improvement & Innovation	15,000-20,000	$44,000
Creation & Implementation of Water GRID & Mist Systems	35,000-50,000	$59,000
Pipeline Improvements & Capacity Increases	500,000-600,000	$64,000
Alternative Fuel & Energy	45,000-50,000	$42,000
Administration/Management	15,000-20,000	$74,000

In order to achieve these benefits we need to have the engineers present to build it we also need educators to be able to inspire the students of today to come up with the next great technological innovation that will change the world. Next, *The Genius Act* will delve into how to incentivize our educators and students alike by creating a new expanded American Opportunity Act in order to spark a new era of economic prosperity. Through education in science, math, and engineering we are able to generate money through ideas and turn those ideas into tangible products that can be sold globally. We also learn to use our valuable natural resources more efficiently to preserve them more for future generations.

IV. The American Opportunity & Education Act of 2013

The Genius Act will request a commission through the Department of Education to create a new class of educators that will earn Genius class distinction. These educators will be eligible to receive Genius class income tax rates as well as eligible for Medical Savings and Retirement Act benefits. They will also be able to set up National Retirement Savings Accounts. Educators in certain fields will receive immediate status distinction these classes include:

- Preschool educators for low income families including those that specialize in language development.
- New math, science, and technology teachers of elementary and secondary students

The Genius Act

- Agriculture and horticulture professors at all community colleges and universities.
- Solar and wind energy installation professionals and instructors at vocational schools.
- Foreign language educators at all levels from elementary to university level professors.
- Electrical and civil engineering professors in urban development including upgrading the nation's Electrical GRID and creation of the Water GRID system.
- Professors at the United States Military Academies and ROTC professors and commissioned officers in military science fields with advanced degrees.

All teachers with at least 5 years of service will receive automatic Genius class status. Pension accounts will have the option of being transferred to the newly created National Retirement Savings Board and will be fully guaranteed based upon years of service. The US treasury will match contributions made by teachers for the first 5 years of the program. Educators will also receive a credit of up to $1,000 or 10% of the amount that they roll into their National Retirement Savings Accounts to a maximum of $10,000. They will also receive a credit equal to 1% of their rollover between 10,001 and $99,999. Withdrawals from these accounts would be taxed at Genius Level tax rates. The penalty rate for withdrawals made before a tax payer is 59 ½ would be lowered to 9%. The tax on excess contributions to retirement plans will be lowered to 1%. Student loan interest payments made will remain an adjustment to income but principal payments on student loans would be subject to the new Genius Act Education credit.

Genius Act Education Credit

As a measure to spur educational advancement and spur job growth the Genius Act will allow for educational credits to income tax that will provide for relief for tax payer's past and present investment in their education. The Genius Act Education Credit will provide a dollar for dollar tax credit up to $5,000 for all educational expenses paid for a taxpayer or dependent child who pursues education in any of the Genius Act fields covered. The credit would be a refundable credit up to 25% of all educational costs paid. Recent college graduates will also be able to deduct 10% of the principal payments made on student loans for a period of 5 years.

In addition the Genius Act Education Credit will include a provision that will allow colleges and universities as well as for-profit educational institutes to receive a refundable credit of 1% of total payments received in order to spur educational advancement. Colleges who agree to freeze tuition rates for a period of 5 years will have their reimbursement rates increase by 1% for the next 5 years. Here is a chart for how the Education credit as well as the reimbursement for students and schools would work:

The Genius Act

Year	Tuition Reimbursement Credit % for College and Universities	Maximum Credit to be received by schools for reimbursement	Student Loan Principal Credit %	Maximum principal repayment amount	Maximum credit for student loan principal payments	Genius Act Education Credit Maximum including Principal Credit
2014	1%	$1 million	10%	$10,000	$1,000	$5,000
2015	2%	$1.1 million	11%	$10,000	$1,100	$5,000
2016	3%	$1.25 million	12%	$10,000	$1,250	$6,000
2017	4%	$1.35 million	13%	$10,000	$1,300	$6,000
2018	5%	$1.5 million	15%	$10,000	$1,500	$7,500

The purpose of this credit will be to provide a reward for educational institutions and students for investments in education. Educational institutions are encouraged to start new schools focusing on horticulture and agriculture, alternative energy engineering and ecology. Parents will be able to withdraw funds from their National Retirement Savings Accounts penalty free to pay for college education for themselves or their dependents that is enrolled in one of these programs.

University Extension High School Program

Prominent universities that surround major metropolitan areas will be encouraged to extend the option to outstanding incoming high school juniors to become their extension university students. These extension schools should attract students from across the metro area as a brand new magnet program with automatic acceptance for students in the top 10% of their graduating class at any school that is rated C, D, or F in the last 3 years in their proficiency ratings. Students will declare their major at this time and spend equal time taking college level pre requisites and high school level mandated courses while earning high school credit and credits toward an associate level degree simultaneously. Universities will be encouraged to develop programs for high school students in the following fields: Nursing, premed, linguistics, early childhood education, engineering, prelaw, and business administration. The goal for these programs will be that students may cut down the amount of time that it takes to earn a bachelor's degree and begin studies on an advanced level degree. Students would become employable faster in order to help pay for their advanced level studies and decrease the need for financial aid or student loans that the students or their parents would have to take out. The Genius Act would encourage the Department of Education to sponsor an initiative for younger graduates to teach linguistics and early childhood education so that younger children may be able to speak multiple languages fluently to become employable worldwide.

The Extension High School Program would also allow students who graduate early to study abroad for their advanced studies and prominent foreign universities would be encouraged to build relationships with promising American high school students with the promise to study abroad once they have received their preliminary degrees. Multiple universities both state university systems and private universities should develop extension high schools in every metro area so that middle schools and traditional high schools may become pipelines of prospective candidates for each school. Extension high schools will be encouraged to hire professors with advanced degrees to teach high school students so that they may accumulate themselves to a higher learning standard before they reach a college campus.

Community colleges will be encouraged to provide continuing education coursework in financial literacy education that would include courses in tax law, investments, and retirement savings. These colleges would also offer courses in foreign language fluency for American students to compete in the global marketplace. Community colleges would give proficiency exams to measure student's success with students receiving a $1,000 refundable tax credit for each course passed and the community college receiving a $250 for each student that successfully passes.

- Colleges will be encouraged to establish new tax-exempt organizations to receive funding and tax credits for continuing education programs. Government agencies and other charitable donors will be given at 10% credit for all donations made to these programs especially towards tuition and materials for low income families. Families who have an adjusted gross income of less than $100,000 will receive a credit of 10% on all contributions made to their dependent's educational savings accounts.

Continuing Education/Financial Literacy Credit

As a part of a larger initiative to increase financial literacy of taxpayers at large, the Department of Education will be funded to provide tax credits to taxpayers who complete financial literacy classes offered through local community colleges. All students who complete classes and pass proficiency exams will receive a dollar for dollar refundable tax credit of $1,000 for each class. The classes that will qualify for the credit are:

- Certified Tax Preparer
- Investments/Retirement Savings
- Foreign language fluency in the following languages: Portuguese, Spanish, French, Japanese, Mandarin(Chinese), Arabic, Russian
- Health Care Administration

Corporations who pay for these classes for their employees or provide the classes through workplace training will receive an additional Education credit of 10% of educational costs paid for employees. Corporations will also receive a credit of $250 for each employee who completes each course including federal state and local government employees.

Genius Act Health Care Education Initiative

The *Genius Act* will propose the formation of a network of research hospitals and surgical centers that will address a wide range of illnesses, injuries, and diseases that threaten to kill Americans and the overall economy at large. The proposal would include a partnership between the Department of Education and the Department of Health and Human Services that will provide tax credits for citizens who pursue education in these fields along with matching grants to educational institutions and endowment funds in order to build and manage these facilities. The proposal would include the following four types of facilities:

- **AIDS/Cancer Research Center-** This center would be charged with researching and developing a cure to these terminal conditions. With centers located near urban centers with the highest rates of these illnesses including Jacksonville, FL, Baltimore, MD, Atlanta, GA, Washington, DC, New Orleans, LA. These cities will be encouraged to work with the state Department of Health and the largest research universities in the area to perform tests using human endocrines such as Human Growth Hormone, Testosterone, and Insulin to stop the carry and spread of these illnesses along with specialized antibiotics to kill bacteria present in the body.
- **The Diabetes Research and Surgery Center-** This hospital will specialize in the treatment and repair of Diabetic conditions including childhood and adult obesity. This hospital would explore the use of endocrines to curb childhood obesity while serving as a treatment for adult diabetes conditions. These hospitals would also develop best practices on performing gastro-intestinal surgeries in order to improve the overall quality of life for all Diabetic patients. They would also work with the Food & Drug Administration to develop new more sophisticated food sources that utilize less sugar intensive ingredients.
- **Women's Wellness Centers-** Each state would be compelled to have at least two locations per state on federal lands that are exclusively devoted to the health and

wellness of women. These centers will focus on: ob/gyn services, family planning and abortion services, oncology and breast health services and dental hygiene. These services would be offered free to all US citizens and resident aliens regardless of age or preexisting conditions and be eligible for hormonal research studies that will include endocrine replacement along with anti-aging medicines.

- **National Sports Science & Surgical Hospital-** The professional sports leagues will work with the Department of Education to create a national research hospital in the advancement of sports science and injury. The hospitals will track athletes from their introduction to sport through their athletic development. Trainers and coaches from all level of sport will be given grants in order to learn training techniques and equipment used in professional sports leagues.

National Football League Select Hospital

The University of Florida in conjunction with the Jacksonville Jaguars will create the first National Football League Select Hospital & Brain Research Centers to study head injuries and overall football injuries and establish principles to provide lifetime health care to any NFL player with at least 5 years of service. Research & Development matching grants would be given to each individual team to establish in their home market within 1 mile of their stadium. They will be encouraged to partner with the leading research university in their home market and contributions made by each university will be matched by the Department of Education and the NFL Players Association. These hospitals shall become training facilities that will employ more surgical physicians, physical therapists and neurologists that will be able to take advantage of Genius class tax rates.

All workers at these hospitals will receive eligibility to receive Genius Tax rates as well as eligible for a refundable tax credit of up to $2,500 or 25% of their total education expenditures.

As a result of the Genius Act Military Budget Reduction Bill detailed later in this book at least two of the federal medical complexes in each state will be on military bases or federally held lands in all of the major metropolitan areas with at 1 million citizens. The presence of these complexes on federal lands will help integrate commerce with lowering healthcare costs and revenue production to provide soldiers and veterans viable opportunities once they leave their service obligations. Next the *Genius Act* will explore how to create Law Enforcement and military jobs while reducing military budget appropriations but creating civilian and private sector jobs for our retiring soldiers and veterans.

V. **Law Enforcement Authorization & Military Budget Reduction Acts**

The Alcohol, Tobacco, Firearms, and Narcotics Authorization Act of 2013

The Genius Act

The *Genius Act* proposes the creation of a plan to fund the Bureau of Alcohol, Tobacco, and Firearms (ATF) along with the Drug Enforcement Agency (DEA) through a revolutionary decriminalization program that will allow the newly formed agency to become a key provider of security and protection of public safety. The ideal configuration of the senior management would be if the President made 3 appointments for co-commissioners and they would be 3 of the 7 members of the newly formed Public Safety Council or to be known as "Crime Commission" with the remaining 4 members of Commission shall include:

- Attorney General of the United States
- Director of the Federal Bureau of Investigation
- Newly appointed National Public Safety Officer/Drug Czar
- Newly appointed Director of Records & Crime Statistics

The "Crime Commission" appointees shall be subject to Congressional confirmation by a simple majority of all Senators. The commission shall meet and have formal minutes taken at least 6 times per calendar year. They will be subject to Congressional hearings semi-annually usually on October 15th and March 15th in order to educate Congress on their progress in crime prevention and to update law makers on budget needs. House and Senate senior leadership shall select members to become part of a standing select committee on Public Safety. The recommendations for each member of the "Crime Commission" are as follows:

- Co commissioner of the ATF: Mayor Rudy Guiliani
- Co commissioner of the ATF: Mayor Michael Bloomberg
- National Public Safety Officer: Gen. Stanley McChristal
- Director of Records & Crime Statistics: Condeleeza Rice

These meetings would be attended by cabinet members as well as the members of the President's executive staff. The agenda and minutes of these meetings will be made available to the public after each semi-annual Congressional hearing in order to facilitate crime prevention across the United States. Each of the officers of the Commission will be responsible for their own direct report officers. They will work with the law enforcement in the FBI and Department of Justice to increase prosecutions in cases of illegal gun possession or gun trafficking and will be responsible for maintaining a gun database for all Genius class citizens.

The National Gun Registry Database

The ATF will maintain a database of all legally held firearms and rifles held by all Genius class citizens. All new guns purchased in the United States by Genius class citizens will be cataloged and matched through the serial number and attached to their Genius ID Number. All weapons must be registered within two years of receiving their Genius class status. Assault rifles that

The Genius Act

have already been purchased may remain with their current owners but all future sales of assault rifles will be subject to a 21 day waiting period. All clips, magazines, or strips may hold no more than 15 bullets on all weapons all cartridges shall have their own serial number for database tracking. Guns will be assigned an owner based their Genius ID number.

The Genius Identification Number (Genius ID Program)

In conjunction with the Social Security Administration, The Department of Homeland Security, IRS, and ATF *Genius Act* will propose the creation and maintenance of a new 13 character Genius Identification Number that will be assigned to all Genius class citizens. It will contain a photo identification that will correspond with the unique 13 digit number assigned to each Genius citizen along with endorsements for each Genius program that the citizen has completed. It will be used by citizens and non-citizens alike and a new number can be reassigned by written request of the holder. The cost of the Genius ID will be $125 for citizens and $1300 for non-citizens. The price for non-citizens or for those requesting "Genius" tax status will increase by $100 every year. In order to renew your Genius ID they must pay their "Genius Society" dues which would amount to 10% of the original price of your membership year with half of the proceeds going to the US Treasury and the other half going to the Genius Society. The program will have a 10 year pilot period in which Congress will reserve the right to commission a research study on the viability of the Genius ID program replacing the Social Security Administration for all income and retirement savings needs. The format for the Genius ID numbers will be as follows:

US Citizens:

13-80-26-98418-00

The first two digits will consist of the year that the holder became eligible for Genius class distinction. The next two digits will be the holder's year of birth followed by the first two digits of their Social Security number. They will then be assigned a random 5 digit Genius number and a two digit job code based on the job class that qualified them for Genius class status.

Foreign Born Resident Aliens/Non-Citizens

13-88-CH-98418-91

The first 4 digits will be the same as US citizens however the next two characters will be a country code for their birth or home nation listed on their application. They will also be assigned a 5 digit Genius number and then and a two digit Genius job class. The above number would be assigned to an applicant from China.

The Genius Act

This number will be used for a number of programs under the Genius Act and will eventually replace the Social Security Number as the main identification number including for tax and retirement savings purposes. For those wishing to have Genius Tax Benefits the cost would be $1300 increasing by $100 per year. Half of the revenue that is received from Genius ID requests will be forwarded to the US Treasury to pay down the federal debt; it will be called the "Debt Society Fund". Renewal dues for each Genius ID will amount to 10% per year of your original purchase price. Half of the renewal dues will also go to the Debt Society Fund. The first program that would utilize the Genius ID number would be the ATF Identification Program.

ATF Identification Program

As a part of the Genius Act the Bureau of Alcohol, Tobacco and Firearms along with the Drug Enforcement Agency will be charged with creating and maintaining a photo identification system that will be mandated in order to purchase any alcohol, tobacco, or firearms. This would also include the purchase of recreational pharmaceuticals that would be legalized as a result of this Act. Citizens who have attained the age of 21 may receive an endorsement from their state agency but all citizens between the ages of 18 and 20 will be required to register with the ATF and complete a Responsible Citizen Consumption Course in order to receive their Identification card. This number will be the same as their Genius ID number that will be used by other agencies within the federal government.

This number will be unique to each citizen and will need to be entered on every purchase made on any of these products. Bulk purchases of any product consisting of 10 cartons or cases of tobacco products, 6 or more cases of beer or liquor, or 3 guns at one time will require an ATF clearance form to be filled out. Consumers would pay $25 to have an endorsement placed on their current identification which would indicate their eligibility to purchase each product. Citizens who are 18-20 would have to pay $100 for their ID card and pay $25 per year in order to renew their license. Citizens who are over 21 will need to renew every 3 years. These fees would go to a newly created Federal law enforcement fund that would facilitate better training of current officers and the hiring of new Public Safety Officers.

Responsible Citizen Consumption Courses

As a new education measure the Genius Act will fund a new revolutionary program that would educate citizens on the dangers and consequences of using all "vice" products. These courses would include education on usage of alcohol, tobacco, firearm, recreational drugs, and sex education. The emphasis of these courses would be focused on the usage of these products as well as the adverse health effects cause by each. The course would be a total of 12 hours and would cover all subjects in a classroom setting along with discussion periods conducted by an instructor broken down in 4 sessions. The class will cost $100 with $60 to be split evenly by the

DEA and the ATF for record keeping and processing and the remaining $40 going to the instructing company for their expenses. All students will be required to complete a proficiency exam that will consist of 100 multiple choice questions evenly divided among the categories covered by the course, with proficiency being achieved with a passing score of 80% or higher. Instruction companies will be required to provide test results of all students passing the course within 30 days of each test taken to the ATF and DEA records division.

Course Curriculum

The course will have a curriculum that will focus on teaching adult citizens the effects of usage of all "vice" products. These products include alcohol, tobacco, and firearms which are currently legal but also will include sexual trade activity, gambling, and recreational drugs which would become legal for Genius ID holders as a result of this act. It will highlight the health care concerns and mortality rates as a result of continued usage of each vice. It will advocate safe gun ownership and require students to sign disclaimer accepting responsibility for improper usage and the possibility of losing possession right if convicted of felony offense in abusing any of the products.

Eligibility Requirements

Residents of al US states and territories who have attained the age of 18 and who have graduated from an accredited high school and are a US citizen or permanent resident will be eligible to apply for a Genius ID card. They must also complete the Responsible Citizen Consumption Course and pass the proficiency exam with a minimum score of 80%. Citizens who are already 21 years of age who are already able to buy tobacco, alcohol, and firearms legally will still need to complete Responsible Citizen Consumption Courses in order to participate in sex trade and gambling activities or to purchase recreational drugs. Genius ID cards will need to be renewed every 3 years. All non-violent felons who have completed their sentences and are willing to pay a one-time $1000 rights reinstatement fee will be able to apply and receive a Genius ID with full eligibility rights. Violent felons would have a 7 year waiting period after they have completed their sentences but would not have the eligibility to purchase firearms without federal district court approval.

Change in Legal Age Requirements

Authorization of the ATF Act will also trigger law changes in the legal possession age of alcohol and firearms. The legal age for these products will be changed to include all 18 year old citizens who have completed high school and who have do not have any felony convictions on their criminal record. Any felonies for use or illegal possession of products will result in a loss of privileges until citizen turns 25 unless granted an exemption by court order. The Genius Act would also make the legal participation age for designated "vice" activities to be 18 years of age and completion of high school education.

Changes in Driving Under the Influence/Driving While Intoxicated/Public Intoxication Laws

For individuals who are 18-20 years old the standard for Driving under the Influence or Driving While Intoxicated shall be changed to include anyone operating a vehicle with a Blood Alcohol Content (BAC) above .05. Any infractions for DUI/DWI while a citizen is 18-20 will result in a suspended or restricted driver's license until the citizen reaches the age of 25 or the completion of 1,000 community service hours.

Legal Age Requirement for Handguns

Under the Genius Act all citizens who meet the conditions for Responsible Citizen Consumption will be eligible to own a handgun. Along with the purchase of a handgun would also include comprehensive liability insurance surcharge of $100 per weapon sold to anyone aged 18-20 or to all non-violent felons who have completed the Responsible Citizen Consumption Course to regain their rights. Handguns purchased by eligible participants would be limited to 12 rounds of ammunition with a felony charged being assigned for carrying more rounds. The Genius Act would also recommend that the age for conceal carry permits be changed also. All guns held by Genius ID holders would be required to be registered under the National Gun Registry database within 90 days of their purchase in order to effectively administer the liability coverage insurance. Any citizen found to be in non-compliance would face a potential loss of Genius ID privileges.

Legalization of "Vice" Activities and Introduction of "Vice Taxes"

As a part of the Genius Act the Responsible Citizen Consumption Course would grant Genius ID holders to participate in activities that were considered illegal or unethical. These activities would the sex trade business, gambling and gaming activity, and usage and sale of recreational drugs. In order to bring those who operate businesses in these fields out of the shadows that they may begin to produce tax revenue and become productive members of society the *Genius Act* aims to make these activities legal by decree of the federal government that they may also be regulated as any other profitable business operation. The taxes collected from these businesses will go toward funding operations in law enforcement, health and human services and toward paying down our growing federal debt. Legalization of these activities will also serve to precipitously reduce crime of all kind as participants have less fear of competition or adverse risks or pursuit by law enforcement.

Sex Trade Activities

The Genius Act

Workers who actively participate in the sex trade would be required to register and receive a Genius ID along with receiving a medical clearance stating that they are disease free. They would be mandated to have health insurance and be tested for all sexually transmitted diseases every 120 days. Activities could only be performed at the newly created S/X chain of hotels that would be eligible to be opened in every metropolitan area with at least 1 million residents. The hotel as well as the worker will each pay a 9% tax on each room rented per day or 5% on extended rentals. Genius ID card holders would pay a minimum of a $9 entry fee to the hotel. Taxes collected will be split between the Department of Health and Human Services and the Department of Justice to fund the Public Safety Officers that would be needed at each facility. Health Care officials will provide free weekly testing to sex workers so that they may display their results inside of their room if needed. All sex workers would be subject to Genius level income tax rates and would eligible to deduct all expense related to their trade from that income and would be eligible to become employees of the hotel and have federal withholding taken out of their paychecks. These chains of hotels would become America's newest enterprise.

Sex Trade Hotels

As a part of the Genius Act sex trade activities would be legalized between Genius class citizens at specific locations. There would be two chains of hotels that would be created as a result of this act that would contain vice activity including gambling and recreational pharmacies. Hotels would only be franchised in metro areas that have at least 1 million residents. Hotels will be limited to 1000 rooms per establishment and each would have standard room rates that start at less than $100 per night. Hotels would be able to lease rooms on short term rates as low as $15 per hour or extended stay rates up to 21 days at a time for as low as $300 per week. Non-resident of the hotel will be required to pay an entry fee of no more than $10. Each hotel will also contain at least 1 restaurant or café and at least one night club in addition to the gaming center and recreational pharmacy. Each hotel must staff at least one Public Safety Officer per 100 guests and revenue agents in the gaming center and recreational pharmacy. Each hotel will be able to facilitate transactions by making workers employees and receiving payments for services before guests are allowed access to residential floors. Workers would have payments debited to their room accounts and receiving cash or check payments once they checkout. The hotel would charge a 10% transaction fee for each exchange; 9% of the transaction fee would go towards the employee's federal withholding balance and 1% for their processing costs. Hotels would also be able to set up mobile credit card processing units for residents. The two hotel chains that would be licensed to be franchised would be S/X Hotel and The Hook-Up Hotel.

The Genius Act

The S/X Hotel would be a live entertainment inspired establishment with club events centered on live performances of sex industry professionals and live music acts. It will be the primary host of sex conventions and various groups of like-minded individuals who want to express their sexual freedom. The hotel will also host media events for television and cable programming and local events to promote a highly social lifestyle.

The Hook-Up Hotel will rival S/X's live entertainment model with its use of all interactive methods to attract clientele. It will encourage its employees to utilize social media to attract friends and online advertising spaces like Craigslist or auction sites like EBay to attract prospective clients. It will maintain a common space that is fully interactive with an internet café with virtual slots and Wi-Fi enabled coffee shops. It will contain smoker's rooms that specialize in flavored hookahs and other products from the recreational pharmacy.

Gambling Activity

The Genius Act will propose the creation of the federal Bureau of Gaming Activity that would control the betting activities that would control internet poker and casino activity as well as live operations at the newly created Genius Gaming centers for Genius ID holders. These centers will be eligible to be opened in metropolitan areas that are larger than 1 million residents. Owners of these establishments will pay modified Genius corporate tax rates:

Modified Tax Rates for Genius Gaming Centers	
Net Income	**Tax Rate**
< $1 million	9%
$1 million -$9.99 million	18%
>$10 million	27%

Genius class gaming customers will also be subject to special tax rates on all winnings and payouts and would be required to input their Genius ID on each transaction. Special Genius tax rates for gambling payouts would be as follows:

Modified Genius Tax Rates for Gambling Winnings	Tax Rates
<$5,000	0%
$5,001-$99,99	9%
$100,000-999,999	18%
$1 million-$9.99 million	27%
>$10 million	33%

The Genius Act

The taxes collected will be split evenly between the Department of Justice to hire more Public Safety Officers and the Department of Treasury to hire more revenue agents and forensic accountants.

Legalizing the Sale & Possession of Recreational Drugs

In an effort to effectively end the "War on Drugs" the ATF will be joined with the Drug Enforcement Agency to legalize drugs federally in specific states by allowing production and sale of narcotics through state run organizations including penitentiaries and distribute drugs nationwide to citizens with Genius ID cards through the United States Postal Service. The following states would be allowed to grow marijuana and sold by state run organizations are: California, Oregon, Washington, Colorado, and Nevada.

States that would be able to manufacture and produce cocaine would be: California, Arizona, Texas, Florida, and Louisiana.

States that would be able to manufacture opiates, heroin, and amphetamines would be: Iowa, Illinois, New York, and Washington, and New Mexico.

Doctors would be licensed to dispense products at "recreational pharmacies" and able to send monthly prescriptions of drugs to patients while paying a special fee per package based upon the state shipped to through the United States Postal Service. The minimum package fee would be $15. Citizens who have taken the Responsible Citizen Consumption Course and have a Genius ID will be eligible to apply for out-of-state residency permits to purchase larger amounts or will have to visit state physician while traveling to receive favored status.

Recreational pharmacies will be set up in cities that have a metropolitan area of at least 1 million residents and no more than 1 mile from the area's drug trauma unit. Most of the pharmacies would be located inside sex trade hotels but can be set up in neighborhoods that are deemed to Genius Business Redevelopment Zones. The following drugs will be legalized under the Genius Act: Marijuana, Cocaine, Heroin, Prescription Strength Opiates, Methamphetamine, MDMA (Molly), K_2 (synthetic marijuana) all will be legalized under the Genius Act. The following are the drugs that are legalized, their price per gram, their corresponding "Vice Tax", and their recommended monthly dosage.

Drug	Price Per Gram	Vice Tax (Percent)	Monthly Dosage/ grams
Marijuana (Generic)	$5	9%	100
Marijuana (Name Brand)	$15	9%	30
Cocaine (generic)	$10	18%	100

The Genius Act

Cocaine (Name Brand)	$30	18%	30
Opiate Pills	$1	27%	300
Methamphetamine	$25	33%	30
Molly/MDMA	$25	27%	30
K$_2$(synthetic cannabis)	$20	27%	30
Crack Cocaine	$60	27%	30

The taxes paid will be collected by DEA revenue agents and the recreational pharmacy operations will be protected by the Public Safety Officers. The revenue collected will be split evenly between the Department of Justice and the Department of Health and Human Services to cover costs for the Affordable Care Act and to fund research studies on addiction and morality rates among drug users. Pharmacies will have to carry bonded liability insurance to cover losses and malpractice lawsuits. All drug manufacturers, pharmacists and salespeople will become Genius class employees and subject to Genius class income tax rates.

The package fee for home delivery through the United States Postal Service will be equal to 1% of the total package or a minimum of $15 through the Special Delivery Unit of the Postal Service. The DEA along with the Post Master Inspector General will hire and retain new revenue agents to monitor these shipments and must be signed for by the Genius ID holder. Package fees will be used to fund Post Office operations and cover budget shortfalls in operations and pension funds. All postal workers would become Genius employees and subject to Genius income tax rates.

Legalization of Genius Performance Enhancers

The Genius Act would propose a research study in conjunction with the University of Florida and the professional sports teams in the state of Florida surrounding the use of a universal performance enhancer called Genius Performance Enhancer (GPE). GPE would be legal for athletes to use in the conditioning and recovery from injury. GPE will be composed of equal parts testosterone (for men) estrogen (for women), insulin, and human growth hormone. It may also contain an anti-inflammatory medication and an antibiotic so that athletes may recover faster from injury. Athletes may participate in weekly blood spinning transfusions where their own blood can be taken from their body supplied with legal endocrines and pure oxygen and fused back into their body weekly. Under a physician's care athletes may transfuse up to 5 gallons of blood per week during their training or off-season. They may also take daily injections of GPE. They may also participate in oxybarric blood transfusions where they are administered transfusions while under general anesthetic in a hypobaric chamber or full oxygen environment throughout the process. They will be able to repeat this process through their training season and up until the end of the first 25% of their games played through the regular season or up until two weeks before a major event or fight. In traveling sports like football, basketball, and baseball all athletes will be subject to a base line test after 25% of the season has been completed which will be made available to medical staff and reporters. They will also be given an "aftershock" test two weeks after the baseline tests to compare their endocrine levels at that point. None of their endocrine levels can spike more than 5% of their "aftershock" without qualifying for a "B" sample test to be requested. If the "B" sample also shows elevated levels that would count as a failed drug test. The player would automatically be suspended for the remainder of his team's season and playoffs. He will be allowed to use GPE during his suspension but must stop after the training season of his team's next season. If an athlete tests positive for any other banned substances he would also be suspend for his team's next season. A second positive test for other banned steroids would result in a lifetime ban from his sport.

GPE can be used by athletes recovering from in-season injuries on a three exception per season rule but the player cannot use his exception on any day that he participates in a game. His doctor must notify the League and media within 24 hours of him receiving blood transfusion or blood spinning treatment. GPE would become legal for use by all professional athletes.

Drug Tariff & Trade Table

In order to reduce crime America's border towns and metropolitan areas the Genius Act would propose a measure that would allow the Mexican and South American drug cartels to sell their products to the federal government through the Drug Enforcement Agency, to retail pharmacies or state run organizations for resale at recreational pharmacies, or directly to customers through mail order. The price would be regulated through each channel and the "vice tariff" would need to be paid after each sale to the Drug Enforcement Agency

This would be the tariff trade rate for cocaine paid by the federal government through the DEA, the price paid by retail pharmacies and wholesalers, and directly to the Genius consumer as well as the amount paid to the DEA as a percentage of each sale based upon quantity sold:

Price Per Kilo (Cocaine)	Retail Direct to customer with packages sent through US Postal	Wholesale to pharmacies and dispensaries for resale	Government Paid by DEA to purchase	Percent Paid to Tariff (% of total sale)
Number of Kilos Sold	$30,000 (base)	$22,000 (base)	$15,000 (base)	
< 1 kg	$30.00/g	$22.00/g	$15.00/g	9%
1 kg-10kg	$27.50/g	$20.00/g	$17.00/g	18%

10-25kg	$25.00/g	$19.00/g	$18.00/g	27%
>25kg	$22.50/g	$18.00/g	$18.00/g	33%

The tariff trade table generic marijuana would be as follows:

Price Per Kilo (Generic Marijuana)	Retail Direct to customer with packages sent through US Postal	Wholesale to pharmacies and dispensaries for resale	Government Paid by DEA to purchase	Percent Paid to Tariff (% of total sale)
Number of Kilos Sold	$1,000 (base)	$700 (base)	$500 (base)	
< 1 kg	$1.00/g	$.70/g	$.50/g	9%
1 kg-10kg	$.80/g	$.70/g	$.50/g	9%
10-25kg	$.70/g	$.60/g	$.50/g	9%
>25kg	$.60/g	$.50/g	$.40/g	9%

For prescription or designer grade marijuana the tariffs would be:

Price Per Kilo (Designer or Prescription Marijuana)	Retail Direct to customer with packages sent through US Postal	Wholesale to pharmacies and dispensaries for resale	Government Paid by DEA to purchase	Percent Paid to Tariff (% of total sale)
Number of Kilos Sold	$5,000 (base)	$3,000 (base)	$2,500 (base)	
< 1 kg	$5.00/g	$3.00/g	$2.50/g	9%
1 kg-10kg	$4.50/g	$2.70/g	$2.50/g	9%
10-25kg	$4.00/g	$2.60/g	$2.40/g	9%
>25kg	$3.50/g	$2.50/g	$2.00/g	9%

The Drug Tariff Table for Injectable Heroin

The Genius Act

Price Per Kilo (Injectable Heroin)	Retail Direct to customer with packages sent through US Postal	Wholesale to pharmacies and dispensaries for resale	Government Paid by DEA to purchase	Percent Paid to Tariff (% of total sale)
Number of Kilos Sold	$80,000 (base)	$55,000 (base)	$40,000 (base)	
< 1oz	$80/g	$55/g	$40/g	9%
1oz-16oz	$75/g	$50/g	$40/g	18%
16oz-1kg	$70/g	$45/g	$35/g	27%
>1kg	$60/g	$40/g	$30/g	33%

The Drug Tariff Table for Methamphetamine

Price Per Kilo (Methamphetamine)	Retail Direct to customer with packages sent through US Postal	Wholesale to pharmacies and dispensaries for resale	Government Paid by DEA to purchase	Percent Paid to Tariff (% of total sale)
Number of Units Sold	$50,000 (base)	$35,000 (base)	$25,000 (base)	
< 1oz	$50/g	$35/g	$25/g	9%
1oz-16oz	$45/g	$30/g	$25/g	18%
16oz-1kg	$40/g	$30/g	$20/g	27%
>1kg	$35/g	$25/g	$20/g	33%

Drug Tariff Trade Table for Synthetic Marijuana (K$_2$) or MDMA

Price Per Kilo (Synthetic Marijuana and MDMA)	Retail Direct to customer with packages sent through US Postal	Wholesale to pharmacies and dispensaries for resale	Government Paid by DEA to purchase	Percent Paid to Tariff (% of total sale)
Number of Kilos Sold	$30,000 (base)	$20,000 (base)	$15,000 (base)	

< 1oz	$30/g	$20/g	$15/g	9%
1oz-16oz	$25/g	$20/g	$15/g	18%
16oz-1kg	$20/g	$15/g	$10/g	27%
>1kg	$20/g	$15/g	$10/g	33%

All orders over 1 ounce or $1,000 must be shipped using US Postal Service pharmaceutical shipping program which would be 1% of the total price of the order or a minimum of $15 per package. Packages would have to originate from the following states to ensure proper packaging protocol: Florida, Louisiana, Texas, Arizona, Nevada, California, Illinois, Michigan or New York. Tariffs collected for drug purchases will be split between the Department of Homeland Security and the Drug Enforcement Agency to hire new border security specialists and revenue agents. Package shipping fees will be paid to cover Postal Service Pension shortfalls.

Canadian and Mexican companies and their employees who wish to trade with Genius class Americans for recreational pharmaceuticals must register and receive a Genius ID and be subject to mandatory income reporting. They would be granted a temporary business visitor's visa after each completed sale in order prospect new business. All foreign Genius class residents will be subject to Genius Income Tax Rates on their American made income.

Creation of the National Public Safety Officer Program

As a part of the ATF Authorization Act there will be a recommendation of creating a new job class of federal law enforcement officers under the direction of the Bureau of Alcohol, Tobacco, and Firearms to be called Public Safety Officers. Unlike traditional police officers and these officers would focus on protecting public safety through education and community involvement. Responsibilities of the Public Safety Officers would include:

- Providing community education on use of Alcohol, Tobacco, Firearms, and recreational drugs through Responsible Citizen Consumption Courses.
- To act as a liaison between the ATF and vendors of each product to ensure responsible record keeping and safety protocol and identification procedures are followed correctly.
- To work with school resource officers to provide periodic protection of elementary and middle schools in their jurisdiction
- To provide protection at "Vice Activity" locations such as Sex Trade Hotels, Recreational Pharmacies, and Genius Gambling establishments.

The Public Safety Officer position will be a GS position with career conditional status after 3 years of service. Veterans will be given preference in filling these positions as they matriculate out of military service and would be subject to Genius level income tax rates. The recommended funding level for these positions would be for 50,000 agents nationwide with an additional 50,000 Drug Enforcement Revenue Agents who will provide security and accounting of the recreational drug market.

Creation of New Treasury Inspector General Revenue Agent Position & Drug Enforcement Revenue Agent Position

In order to regulate new vice activities that were previously illegal it will be necessary to hire more law enforcement agents who specialize in tax and income reporting. These agents will be charged with creating an environment where citizens feel comported to report their income and pay their fair share of taxes on that income. These revenue agents will be charged with collecting vice taxes and making sure that deposits are made to the proper agencies or to the Treasury in a timely matter. They will work with these tax payers on ensuring timely filing on proper tax documents. The initial funding for staffing this position should include at least 50,000 agents to adequately cover the United States. Recreational pharmacies and sex trade hotels will be required to staff agents on a fulltime off duty basis to protect operations. Genius gaming centers will have agents as well as Public Safety Officers staffed to ensure peace and proper accounting on a nightly basis. All employees under this newly created job class will be eligible for Genius class status and would be subject to Genius class income tax rates. We must now examine how to positively employ all military personnel and honorable veterans while reducing our military budget in this postwar society.

Military Budget Reduction & Reform Act of 2013

As an effort to employ all of those who have served our country honorably while reducing our military budget the Genius Act has created a solution to cure the problems that ill the Department of Defense as they find creative ways to employ all of their active personnel while setting them on a prosperous path of employment as they transition into civilian life. The provisions of Military Budget Control Act will recreate the Department of Defense with Genius class jobs that will have unemployment opportunities for all veterans. As America shifts its focus and resources from foreign based wars the Defense Department shall appropriate funds used for military operations into new projects that will provide environmental and economic security for the United States and all of its strategic allies. This Act will incentivize military and support personnel by providing Genius class tax favored status to specialized job classes as well as all war veterans who have at least 3 years of service. The following jobs classes will automatically receive "Genius" classification:

- Linguistics or translator specialists
- Counterintelligence and clandestine operations
- Unmanned aircraft pilots and operators

The Genius Act

- Agricultural engineers (new job class)
- Energy engineers (new job class)

The Genius class distinction will also be bestowed upon all active duty, veteran, and civilian personnel who participate in the Master Growth Food Project. All employees will be eligible to participate in the Medical and Retirement Savings Act program as well as start National Retirement Accounts. The Department of Defense shall commission a comprehensive feasibility study to determine the effectiveness of the Master Growth Food Project on each military base and outpost both foreign and domestic. As we end the wars in Iraq and Afghanistan our war fighting personnel will need to be trained in new job classes so that America can meet its protection needs and our veterans can meet their employment needs.

As our soldiers return stateside we will need to upgrade their skill sets to include training in two areas of critical need for the future: energy and agricultural security. These skills will become the job classes of the future as they can be deployed in military and humanitarian aid. The Genius Act will create two new job classes to accomplish these goals. The two new job classes would be Agricultural Engineer and Energy Engineer. The Corp of Engineers will develop a college level curriculum to train enlisted men and officer trainees in either field and offer enhanced GI Bill funding for veterans or retirees to enroll in degree seeking programs in each field. Veterans who complete Corp Engineer training or who receive a degree in the field of study will be given preference in receiving civilian status jobs in maintaining the project.

Agricultural Engineers will engage in training techniques that will include soil irrigation and engineering as well as hydroponic growing that will allow them to secure and maintain America's food sources. They will grow fruits and vegetables, dairy poultry and other protein staples. They will work alongside civilian management and their own commanding officer administration to provide security to the project. The soldiers will provide leadership and training of military standard operations to other personnel working at the project which would include local and migrant workers and inmates assigned to the Project.

The second job class to be created would be that of an Energy Engineer. The Corp of Engineers will create an alternative energy source program that will develop soldiers' aptitudes in maintaining energy independence for all military posts foreign and domestic. The program will focus on solar and wind energy sources that will be portable and easily assembled in a mass fashion. The Corp will bring in civilian experts to provide state of the art technology to implement each base's energy needs. The Department of Defense shall offer advanced extension courses to expedite expansion of enlistee's knowledge base. Enlistees in each program will work alongside linguistics and counterintelligence specialists to improve relations at all project sites. The will be encouraged and incentivized to learn languages and acquire knowledge on intelligence gathering techniques to help diffuse security threats. This will facilitate the development of the Goodwill Food & Energy Project in foreign outposts. Stateside, soldiers will provide for the creation of the National Food Complex to provide food staples at military bases for all Genius class citizens.

Creation of the National Food Complex

The Department of Defense along with the Department of Agriculture will to create an open air marketplace for fresh and organic foods including poultry, dairy, and seafood products made available to Genius class citizens on military bases and other federally appropriated lands. Wal-Mart and other large retailers would compete to form public-private partnerships with the federal government to provide logistical support to these food complexes and allow them to set up Wal-Mart Food Centers on military bases and use Public Lands to build Food Complexes in the inner city. Food Complexes would be built inside of larger Federal Business Complexes that would include a Healthcare Complex, and the National Farmer's and Butcher's Market, retail stores and financial institutions for public use.

The Goodwill Food & Energy Project

The Department of Defense along with the Departments of Agriculture and Interior will develop a partnership with allied foreign governments where we currently have military bases and consulates. In order to foster peace and prosperity with all nations the United States would agree to remove military personnel in favor of building sustainable food and energy sources in these locations. The locations will be securely maintained with military personnel who have now been trained to refurbish these sites to now include Master Growth Food projects that will include fruits and vegetables as well as dairy and poultry products if readily available. These products will utilize local labor forces to staff the project to work alongside military and civilian personnel who will be trained by the Army Corp of Engineers. Food produced by the project will be provided to low income families and those in temporary and refugee housing due to war displacement or religious persecution. Surplus products produced will be provided to local markets in the region to subsidize food costs and spur economic growth. US multinational corporations will be able to bid with foreign governments to develop exportable food products from these regions.

The Department of the Interior will provide technological expertise in developing alternative energy sources including wind, solar, and hydro energy to power these projects and also develop lasting renewable energy sources for the surrounding communities. The Department of the Interior and the Corp of Engineers will work along with each nation's energy department to facilitate the placement of Energy Engineers to install and maintain these new energy developments. The United States will initially develop these projects on lands leased or owned by the government but will also push for projects to be developed in war torn regions with large settlements of displaced people. There will also be a proposal to expand projects into less developed nations in the near future with an emphasis on establishing these projects in Central & South American nations and African provinces.

Corporations who participate in the program will be subject to Genius corporate tax rates on all activities associated with the program. All employees of these corporations will also be subject to Genius income tax rates. Public service grants will be provided to companies who train and employ former military personnel in civilian management capacities. These companies will also employ members of the newly formed Farm Corp organization and also non-violent felons rehabilitated under the Prison Reform Act to be later detailed in the Genius Act. Local and migrant project workers as well as deported resident aliens and felons employed by the program in their home country will be eligible under the Immigration Reform Act to receive citizenship status after 5 years of service to the program and making a requisite donation to the Society Debt Fund.

The Goodwill Farming Corporation of America (Farm Corp)

In an effort to create opportunity for America's youth to experience an international lifestyle at an early age the Genius Act recommends the creation of the Goodwill Farming Corporation of America. Farm Corp will be a volunteer based agricultural program that will allow the military along with other invested partners to set up long term food and energy projects in emerging and developing nations while promoting peace and prosperity. American youth who have graduated high school or rising seniors with exceptional business or agricultural acumen and are willing to achieve language proficiency to fit one of the Farm Corp's project needs will be able to apply for the program. They will receive a stipend of $33,000 a year to cover college costs and personal expenses while learning the intricacies of the culture and farming prospects in their project nation. They will also make recommendations of new crops that could be grown in the project and learn alternative energy sourcing techniques and how to make the energy sources portable. They will be able to receive significant college credit for work completed in the project so that they may complete their post graduate studies expeditiously and move into project management if they desire. The minimum commitment to the project would be for 3 years but the recommended length of service would be 5 years with students accomplishing educational goals faster in order to allow them the freedom to serve at an integral part of their life. It will give the opportunity to claim their stake at the American dream and a chance to interact with the best and brightest that the world has to offer.

The Genius Act

Part 2: Getting Out of the Shadows

In this section of *Genius Act* we will explore to return America to a place of full employment and beyond while providing a new level of prosperity for 13 million workers who have been "lost in the shadows." First we will look into a comprehensive immigration policy that will put hard working immigrants to work legally so that they may be able to support their families here and abroad while ensuring they have a clear concise path to legal citizenship. We then will delve into reforming America's broken prison and probation and parole policies that make it difficult if not nearly impossible for prisoners and felons to support their families and lead to a high rate of recidivism and high rates of generational poverty and incarceration as children explore a life of crime without proper parental guidance. The Genius Act aims to be the guiding light to prosperity as we end the shadows of poverty.

VI.   The American Dream Immigration Reform Act of 2013

With at least 11 million residents here in America illegally and countless more whose status is in limbo either by no fault of their own or due to some legal or technical issue we must develop a policy that will allow all of residents to live out the American Dream. As a part of the Genius Act would be a proposal to provide improved clarity in the immigration policy. This proposal would be made to the Department of Immigration and Customs Enforcement and the Department of Homeland Security to make for a collaborative policy implementation. The American Dream Act will provide a path for citizens of the world to follow in pursuit of American citizenship and prosperity. Undocumented residents including those covered under DACA and the Dream Act along with migrant farmers and extraordinary personnel will be given preference in citizenship grants. They will be included in the development of the Genius Society and given a greater responsibility in order to maintain their rights. The following will be the guidelines for immigrants achieving the American Dream.

Undocumented Residents currently living in the United States

Persons living in the United States without a valid resident visa will be allowed to apply for work visas through the DACA program. After obtaining work permits, workers will be subject to Genius level income tax rates. Corporations will be encouraged to create new entities specifically to employ these workers as they will also receive Genius level corporate income tax rates. Workers will receive a permit that will be valid for 5 years. During that time frame recipients will need to remain employed for 17 of the 20 quarters that the permit covers. For any quarter that the permit holder is not employed they will be expected to remain in contact with their immigration officer and will be expected to complete at least 20 volunteer hours per month for every month that they are unemployed. It is preferred that they complete their volunteer service in the Master Food Program.

Workers will be required to file timely tax returns for each year they are employed. They will commit no felony offenses or face possible revocation of their permit with violent felony offenders receiving automatic revocation and possible deportation. Drug and human trafficking offenders will also face automatic revocation. Drug and sex trade workers would be required to register with the Genius Society in order to gain entry in the United States.

Children of Undocumented Residents Living in United States

Dependent children of work permitted or permanent resident aliens will receive citizenship status if they attain the age of 18 and have received a high school diploma. Children who are dependents that have already attained the age of 18 will receive citizenship status upon obtaining a college degree or vocational certification, or enlistment in the Armed Forces, Peace Corp, or newly formed Farm Corp. All children born to these dependent children on American soil or any of its territories shall be naturalized as American citizens. Children who attain the age of 18 who do not receive a high school diploma and are not enrolled in a vocational program will be required to apply for a work permit within 90 days of their 18th birthday. Each working family will also be able to sponsor one non-resident family member who will remain as a household worker or child care provider.

Migrant Farmers working in United States

In order to boost America's agricultural dominance and to provide opportunities for agricultural workers with extraordinary farming talent agro business entities will be encouraged to hire migrant farm workers to work on Master Growth Food Projects inside the United States. These corporations will be responsible for providing housing, medical coverage, transportation, and required to pay these workers equal to the "Genius wage". These positions will be subject to Genius level income tax rates and the corporations will qualify for Genius level corporate tax rates if they choose. These workers will be required to file timely tax returns each year that they are employed and will be subject to Medical & Retirement Savings Act benefits. They will be registered in the Genius Society and their "Society Debt" will be paid by the company that sponsors them while being repaid by payroll deduction. Work permits will be valid for 5 years and holders will be required to be employed for 17 of the 20 quarters that the permit covers unless they receive an official exemption by their sponsoring company. Permit holders who become involuntarily unemployed during any quarter will receive credit for a working quarter by completing 60 volunteer hours in the Master Food Program. After completion of work requirements applicants may request that their spouse and dependent children join them to reside in the United States with a corresponding application and "Society Debt" fee attached.

Local farmers of foreign nations working on Master Food Projects

The Genius Act

In an effort to improve foreign relations with allied nations the US Department of Agriculture will offer a path to citizenship for local farmers of foreign nations who offer their services to Goodwill Food & Energy Projects for a period of 5 years. They will work alongside American volunteers from the Farm Corp who will help them overcome language barriers as the American volunteers immerse themselves in their language and culture while they perform their service. Farmers who perform exemplary service and are willing to take "Genius" wage jobs at Master Food Projects in the United States will be able to apply for their nuclear family to join them in the United States. The participants in this program will be subject to Genius Level tax rates and will become a part of the worldwide Genius class eligible to receive Genius wages in any country they work in.

Genius of field educators and entrepreneurs

The American Dream Immigration Act shall include a provision to allow all persons who are considered among the top 1% of educators in their field of study will be given authorization to enter the United States with the promise of citizenship if they are employed for 5 years and meet citizenship guidelines including filing timely tax returns. These educators will be invited to join the Genius Society and subject to Genius level income tax rates and eligible for Medical and Retirement Savings Act benefits. Entrepreneurs who own businesses that have proven profits of $250,000 a year for at least the past 3 years or who have sponsored financing from a Genius Society organization will be granted permits to work in the United States and will be eligible for Genius class tax rates on their employment income for a period of 5 years. They will have the flexibility of applying for citizenship or maintaining their current citizenship and receive an extension of their sponsored status

Military personnel employed on Master Food or Goodwill Food & Energy Projects

Special provisions will be made to allow those that agree to receive US military training and work as security personnel in foreign Master Food Projects or Goodwill Food & Energy Projects to be eligible to apply for American citizenship after 5 years of service to the program. They will be subject to Genius level tax rates on income earned while working inside the United States and subject to GATT tax rates on income earned while in their home country or on other Master Food Projects. Workers will also have the opportunity to apply for their dependent children and spouses to join them in the United States and be eligible for citizenship provided they meet Genius Act standards and are able to pay the "Society Debt" fee.

Students who receive advanced degrees or who receive highest honors distinction in Math, Science, Engineering, linguistics, and Agriculture

The Genius Act

Foreign born students who receive education in the United States will be eligible to receive a work permit that would automatically lead to citizenship if they remain to receive an advanced degree in the fields of math, science, engineering, technology, linguistics, or agricultural or energy science. The permit would be valid for 5 years to allow them to advance their education and any income earned would be subject to Genius income tax rates and they would be eligible for Medical and Retirement Savings Act benefits. They would need to file timely tax returns and remain felony free to receive citizen status.

Nonviolent felony deportees and detainees

Undocumented residents who face deportation or are in long term detention will be granted amnesty to join the Master Food Project in order to provide service eligible to regain citizenship status. Detainees must agree to return to their home country for a minimum of 3 years in order to complete their service before they can reapply for entry into the United States. Felons may also do service in foreign Master Food projects or Goodwill Energy Projects and after 5 years of service they may reapply for residency and citizenship rights.

Drug Trade and Sex Trade Workers

Workers in the drug traded and sex trade industry who were previously undocumented or operating with invalid visas will be given amnesty to join the Genius Society and receive a Genius ID after taking a Responsible Citizen Consumption Course will be given a 1 year work permit to perform their services in the United States but must register with the local sex trade hotel or recreational pharmacy within 30 days of receiving their work permit. They will be subject to Genius income tax rates and must file their tax returns within 90 days of the expiration of the license and their license cannot be renewed until their tax return is filed.

Genius Textile Program Workers

In order to battle deplorable working conditions of "sweatshops" in the textile and manufactured goods industry the Genius Act will recommend the Genius Textile Workers Program for the top 1% of textile workers worldwide to join the Genius Society and work in American built factories and receive Genius wages while better factories are built in their home countries. Up to 100,000 workers per year will receive 5 year work permits to live and work in the United States under the supervision of their sponsors. There will be tax credits given to corporations who open factories in Genius Business Redevelopment zones. Workers will be subject to Genius income tax rates and will be eligible for Medical & Retirement Savings benefits. The Commerce Department will propose trade treaties that will make their pay standard worldwide so that we can fight the inequality of conditions that exist in factories in lesser developed nations.

VII.   Prison Reform & Reconciliation Act of 2013 & "New Freedom Budget" Initiative

New Freedom Budget Initiative

In an effort to combat poverty in all communities but especially minority communities that have been ravaged by the "War on Drugs" and the rampant criminality and systemic poverty that it has produced. The Genius Act seeks to propose a new Freedom Budget Initiative to replace the lost policy of the early 1960's. This Freedom Budget seeks to empower those already deemed to be criminals and have suffered through long term incarceration or supervised release under the tyrannical justice system. This initiative seeks to instill confidence that Black and brown prisoners that they can rejoin society at large and can become productive members of the Genius Society. The Great American economy was built on the backs of strong Black and Brown men and their disappearance from being productive members of the economy has led to the demise of the economy and society in general. The prison system has become nothing more than a holding pen effectively putting a stop to lives' where a pause would have been more effective. This Freedom Budget aims to set up a payment system that will allow those incarcerated to start to live again.

While paying their debt to society, prisoners need to know that they can also acquire skills that will allow them to take care of their families, make restitution to the victims of the crimes they committed, and gain back some of the personal freedoms that they enjoyed in the outside world. They will become responsible for their own destiny and be able to reduce their sentences by making responsible choices on how to reduce their debt to society. They will be able to gain basic rights to do things such as communicate through technology so that they may remain relevant members of the world during their incarceration. This will provide them with sufficient motive to utilize their entrepreneurial skills and work ethic to become providers again in communities where economic support is vital and truly needed to end the cycle of generational poverty.

This new "Freedom Budget" will become the basis of a new "trickle out" economic theory where those who should have been shifting the pistons of our economy but could not due to long or perpetual incarcerations can now make their rightful contribution to a new era of prosperity. They will be able to join the Genius working class which will allow them to acquire skills in the fields of study that they are already familiar with and be able to be gainfully employed once their incarceration ends. Corporations will be able to access a steady stable supply of workers that will allow them to invest their resources on low risk highly productive workers.

Each individual's Freedom Budget would be as follows:

The Genius Act

25% of earnings would go to the Debt Society Fund

25% of their earnings would go to their Family Support Account or Victim's Restitution Fund if their crime had victims.

25% of earnings to alternate account if they have victims and family obligations

25-75% would go to their personal use commissary account or to purchase time off of their sentences.

Bonuses would be given to inmates who achieve proficiencies in languages, financial literacy, or who receive agricultural or energy engineer designations. Inmates will be able to join the Genius class after they are released and will be employed by Master Food Projects and Goodwill Food & Energy Projects. All income will be subject to Genius income tax rates and will be eligible for Medical & Retirement Savings Act benefits. Now we will explore the Prison Reform Act that will give those incarcerated the freedom to live despite their current situation.

Prison Reform & Reconciliation Act of 2013

The Genius Act shall make provisions for Federal Corrections Institutes (FCI) to employ residents at the Master Growth Food Projects. Prisoners will be engaged in growing fruits, vegetables, and meat and protein products. They would also have the opportunity to grow recreational drugs if those products are legalized under the Genius Act. Prisoners who volunteer to join this project will have the opportunity to commute part of their sentences as well as enroll in programs like the Family Support Fund and the Victim's Restitution Fund that will allow them to earn Genius wages while incarcerated. They will be able to provide financial support to their families and to the families of the victims of their crimes as they pay their debt to society.

This Act will create agricultural projects that use alternative energy sources such as wind, solar, and hydroponic feeds so that these facilities can become energy independent. These facilities will also be connected to the Water GRID to lessen the environmental impact that these projects may impose. They will also be involved in growing all natural feed products for the animals and livestock grown on the project. This act will also provide for Genius wage readjustment jobs to prisoners as they transition back into society. There will also be a Debt to Society Corporation that will be charged with the management and administration of this program. These jobs will be eligible for Genius tax rates and any corporation that hires workers through this program will be eligible for Genius corporate rates. Inmates will also be eligible for Medical & Retirement Savings Act benefits.

The Master Growth Food Project will be enacted under provisions in this Act. The project will utilize inmates, migrant workers, military and civilian personnel to maintain the project.

The Genius Act

Inmates will be the base workforce in all domestic projects. The project will use traditional and non-traditional growing techniques and methods to teach prisoners how to become independent farmers and agriculturalists. They will learn techniques in soil and crop rotation so that they may take advantage of the best growing seasons for land that is available to them. They will also learn best practices to grow and manage livestock of poultry, beef, and pork to be sold at local meat and dairy markets for profit. They will learn how to maintain and harvest foods to be sold at the newly created National Farmer's Market that will provide subsidized goods for citizens to purchase locally at weekend open air markets. The revolutionary program will not end there.

The Master Growth Food Project will create indoor growth facilities for plants and animals to expand growth cycles for each while using alternative energy methods. These indoor facilities will use solar panels and wind energy to power the facilities and experiment with hydroponic growth methods to improve organic food availability of consumable foods for consumers as well as for feeding of livestock to be consumed. Foods grown will be first made available to the prison facilities so that they may become self-sufficient. Any excess products will then be provided to state and local prison systems at subsidized rates to minimize costs. Remaining products will then be made available to large retailers or local markets, or provided to goodwill efforts to needy families. As these farms grow and produce more excess products it will necessitate the formation of the National Farmer's Market & Butcher Store.

The National Farmer's Market & Butcher Store shall be created and managed by the Debt to Society Corporation, a new Genius class employer. The corporation will be funded through block grants from the Department of Justice and the Department of Agriculture in lieu of food assistance grants. Prisoners will be paid on the "Genius wage scale" equivalent to a minimum of 60% of the Genius minimum wage or $9.00 per hour or higher. Prisoners will have the option to use this pay to purchase goods through their canteen accounts or to have days removed from their sentences on a daily rate purchase system. They will also have the option to divert funds from their account to their families or dependent children through the newly created Family Support Act. Prisoners will also be eligible to participate in a profit sharing program that will be determined on Debt to Society's annual profits. They can opt to have bonuses directed to their cash account balance, Family Support account, or to their National Retirement Savings Account. We will now examine how inmates will use these jobs to pay off their debts: Debt to Society, Debt to Family, and Debt to their Victims.

Debt to Society

Each inmate employed at Master Growth Food Projects will become a member of the Genius Society. As a member of the society they will be responsible for contributing 25% of their salary to their Debt to Society each year up to $3300. In their first year $1300 of that debt will go to the Society Debt Fund. The remaining $2000 will go towards their purchase of days to commute their sentence at a rate of $40 per day totaling 50 days. After their first year their dues to the Society will be lowered to $300 with the remaining $3000 going to purchase days off of their sentence totaling 75 days. They may purchase up to 75 more days per year after they have met their obligations to the Family Support Act and/or the Victim Restitution Fund if they have those obligations. By joining the Genius Society, inmates will also secure a future for themselves once they are released from prison.

The Debt to Society Corporation will enroll inmates in Genius wage readjustment jobs that will allow inmates to earn full Genius class wages once they have served their sentences or have paid to have a significant portion of their sentences commuted. These jobs will be subject to Genius income tax rates and inmates with non-violent offenses will have their rights restored if they remain employed in these jobs and commit no further felony offenses for 5 years after their release. Recently released felons and parolees shall be eligible to receive housing assistance near FCI locations in order to participate in the program and enroll in other rehabilitative services to ease their readjustment into society.

States may apply for block grants to implement these programs at the state and local levels in lieu of penal outlays provided from the Department of Justice. The Debt to Society Corporation shall qualify for Genius level corporate tax rates and by proxy allow auxiliary and subsidiary employers to be set up by state corrections facilities.

Debt to Family (Family Support Act)

In an effort to correct years of systemic and generational poverty by families who are ripped apart by prison sentences by the household breadwinners, the Genius Act proposes the creation of the Family Support Act as a part of the Prison Reform & Reconciliation Act. Inmates who have dependent children who receive SNAP benefits or who are enrolled in Medicaid will be required to have an allotment of 25% of their income to go towards a family support account set up by the state child support enforcement agency where that dependent child lives. The income will go to offset the cost of benefits that state or federal agencies provide to that child's family each month. Excess cash benefits provided by the inmate will be forwarded to the benefit debit card that the custodial parent already maintains. Inmates will also have the option to purchase gift cards or gift certificates to large retailers through their canteen accounts to be sent to the child or custodial parent in addition to any cash benefits provided. Inmates will also have the option to set up educational savings accounts to be placed in a trust until the child turns 18. All payments made to Family Support Accounts will be made with pretax dollars.

Debt to Victims (Victim Restitution Fund)

The Genius Act

Inmates who are imprisoned for violent crimes against others or on financial crime felonies where personal losses occurred may be held responsible for a debt to those victims. The Victim's Restitution Fund will be established to cover those debts. If victims make claim against an inmate's income he may be required to pay the victim or make a donation of up to 25% of their salary to the Victim Restitution Fund. Standards will be set by the courts for the cost of each claim per crime committed and victims would be notified by mail to ascertain if they would be interested in filing a claim against individual defendants. They will have the option of receiving a cash payment directly from the inmate's salary. They also can elect to have that payment made in their name to the Victim Restitution Fund and receive a charitable contribution credit for that donation. After paying off their debts inmates need to have the tools to successful in society and embark on a journey that will stop the cycle of recidivism and perpetual incarceration.

Genius Society Jobs & Master Food and Energy Projects

In an effort to unlock the limitless potential of inmates who have been held back by the scourge of incarceration the Genius Society will give prisoners varied work experience to ensure their success once they have completed their sentence. They will be given jobs in Master Food Projects working along with immigrant farmers, active military personnel and veterans to protect and grow America's food and energy sources. They will become the frontline soldiers in America's war on poverty as we move through the 21st century and away from the war on terror. They will be trained to be agricultural and energy engineers the same as our veterans and retirees so that they may be able to provide an able support system to our war weary veterans returning from multiple deployments and suffering through their own problems such as post-traumatic stress. They will learn languages in order to ease the transition for our immigrant populations working on the project so that they can build camaraderie around the same goal: striving to return America to greatness. That aura of greatness will not be limited to our borders. Prisoners will also be given the opportunity to showcase our spirit of humanitarianism and giving by participating in Goodwill Food & Energy Projects on foreign lands.

Under provisions of a Genius Act Trade Treaty prisoners who have been trained to work on Master Food & Energy Projects will be eligible to work on Goodwill Food &Energy projects on foreign lands. As we reduce our military budgets that fund war operations and reallocate those funds to humanitarian and goodwill efforts we can produce results that require minuscule investment as opposed to our war strategy. They will work with local farmers, military personnel, and members of the Farm Corp to establish and maintain these projects with our strategic economic allies. The projects will focus on emerging and developing nations who are in dire need of humanitarian food and energy support. However, there will be projects opened in war torn nations and settlements of temporary and interment housing. Prisoners will demonstrate to the world that America is not only the land of second chances, but truly the "Land of Opportunity". Here is a look at the job creation that would result from the implementation of the Prison Reform Act and the Master Food and Energy Projects:

Direct Jobs Created(type)	# of jobs created	Average Income of jobs created
Inmates	1,600,000-2 million	$27,500-$38,000
Support Staff (prison local)	200,000-350,000	$48,500-$61,000
Support Staff (foreign projects)	100,000-150,000	$36,000-$42,000
Military Staff (Active Duty)	50,000-65,000	$51,000-$61,000
Military Staff (Civilian)	150,000-175,000	$58,000-$77,000
Administrative Staff	5,000-7,500	$69,000-81,000
Indirect Jobs Created		
Solar & Alternative Energy Sources	75,000-100,000	$38,000-$47,000
Construction & Engineering	20,000-25,000	$44,000-$52,000
Cooperative Farmers	220,000-250,000	$58,000-$75,000
Farm Corp (nonprofit)	250,000-300,000	$33,000

As you can see the inmates can become the driving force in a "trickle out" economic policy that focuses on putting the "hidden workforce" back to work. They can learn skills that are employable worldwide and they will have a seamless transition into the Genius Society. State and local agencies can use revenue produced from these programs to fund educational programs that will reverse the "schools to prisons" pipeline that currently exists and use the labor of current prisoners to invest in the future.

Genius Drug Trade Worker Program

As outlined in the ATF Authorization Act prisoners will also receive training in the manufacture and sale of recreational pharmaceuticals including marijuana and cocaine through the Master Food Project. They will have the opportunity to take Responsible Citizen Consumption Courses while incarcerated and produce products that can be sold at recreational pharmacies. Once prisoners receive their Genius ID they will become registered Drug Trade Workers with the ability to sell products to other Genius ID holders or work at recreational pharmacies once they are released. The Debt to Society Corporation will make a contribution of at least 10% of drug revenue to educational initiatives through the Department of Education. State and local agencies will be able to use revenues produced to cover budget shortfalls and fund educational programs including after-school programs. As the slaves led the revolution to end slavery and the "bootleggers" led the economic revolution after the Great Depression may the prisoners lead the revolution to end the "War on Drugs" by giving us a working example of how to end the prohibition on recreational drugs and lead us to the Glory Road to economic prosperity in the 21st Century and producing a new generation of entrepreneurs free from the regulatory controls of law enforcement.

"Freedom Riders" Program

As a part of a proposed brand marketing opportunity for American automakers called "Freedom" brands, which would combine gas combustion and alternative fuel options with electric and solar technology to make the most fuel efficient cars in the world. Prisoners would acquire the skills necessary to build these cars while they are incarcerated. General Motors GM® and other American automakers would be encouraged to build factories or assembly plants inside or close to correctional facilities that will allow these cars to be completely American made and assembled. Prisoners would enter a specialized training program to build cars under the "Freedom" brand that would be sold to low income or credit challenged individuals. Top performers would be invited to join a chapter of Genius Society sponsored by the United Auto Workers and eventually join the Genius Society and earn Genius wages. Workers who perform 5 years of service to the program will receive a vehicle that they built upon their release.

As we have now explored all actions necessary to bring America to "beyond full employment" status we will now delve into providing equal opportunity to all workers, entrepreneurs, and corporate entities to make a difference in the Genius Society. Part 3 will cover Genius Society Wage and Tax Reforms that will allow this new era of economic prosperity to continue perpetually while eliminating bubbles by making the workforce participation independent of financial industry practices and allowing workers and entrepreneurs to be independently financed.

Cadillac Jets & Genius Airlines

The Genius Act will include a provision to create a new manufacturer of luxury jet airplanes. The ownership of this company would be split evenly between The US Treasury, Boeing, and General Motors. The planes would be designed and manufactured in plants based in Detroit, Chicago, Indianapolis, and Dayton, OH. Income from this joint venture would be subject to Genius level income tax rates for the corporations and their employees. Penal workers would enter a specialized training program to become Genius Society workers building and maintaining these aircraft. All sales and lease agreements would be subject to a flat 9% transaction tax and fuel surcharges would be taxed at 9% on all purchases.

The Genius Act

Part 3: G.E.N.I.U.S. Wage Act & Genius Act Tax Reforms

VIII.   The G.E.N.I.U.S. Wage Act of 2013 & The Genius Society

After exploring all of the options necessary to bring the nation to full employment and beyond the Genius Act, aims to delve into actions necessary to avoid bubbles in the workforce market while insuring that there is always room for workforce expansion and shared prosperity among all workers. Instead of racing to the bottom to find the lowest wage that companies can pay workers to achieve maximum profitability *The Genius Act* instead aims to achieve maximum productivity by capturing each worker's Genius ambitions. Employees will know that in addition to a safety net that will catch them if they were to fail from their peak; there will also be a rising floor that will allow them to ascend without the threat of them losing their balance before they reach their limitless potential.

The G.E.N.I.U.S Wage Act of 2013

The cornerstone of the Genius Act is to create an equal opportunity for the accumulation of wealth, education, and prosperity. After addressing all of those issues we will now address the most pressing problem of poverty: depressed wages and the rise in the cost of living for those that can least afford it. As more workers join the worldwide workforce the disparity of wages has become more apparent as the competition for open positions has become fiercer. The way to battle and defeat this problem is to create an equalized worldwide wage system for all workers. That system is **G**reat **E**mployment **N**ational **I**ndustrial **U**niversal **S**ystem or **G.E.N.I.U.S.** system for all workers covered under this Act. The GENIUS system will create a minimum wage for all workers who acquire training and education necessary to perform their job's skill set. This wage system will be applicable to workers whether they choose to join labor organizations or not. However, it would be recommended that workers of all job classes organize and become a part of the Genius Society, a newly organized labor union with a higher wage scale for all workers who join the union. As the saying goes "the rising tide raises the level of all ships" the GENIUS wage would raise incomes for all workers. As we address the salary disparities of those at the bottom we will begin to expand the incomes of small business owners, entrepreneurs, and others who aspire to join the middle class or beyond. Workers would have the opportunity to patronize businesses or have businesses expand as their wealth grows, and with them so would the wealth of their communities and that of society at large. We will delve into Genius Society wages later but here are the Genius wages for non-Genius Society workers:

$9.00 per hour

This would be the minimum hourly wage for all workers worldwide no matter their job class. These job classes would include agricultural and farm workers, tip wage employees, and penal workers (prisoners). Workers in these classes will have their earnings reported on a newly created W-2GE. This new form will resemble a standard W-2 form but will have modifications to line items that will be added as a result of the adoption of the Genius Act. Line items for Social Security wages and Social Security taxes will be replaced by line items indicating the newly created Retirement Savings Act which will be detailed later in the Genius Act tax reforms. Genius class workers who have worked in both systems would be subject to a modified Social Security benefit once they reach retirement age. The payroll deduction for the Retirement Savings Act would be 4.5% of pretax income as opposed to 6.2% under the Social Security payroll deduction. The income threshold on Retirement Savings Act withholdings however will be on all income up to $250,000, in addition there will be a 2.5% withholding on income between $250,001 and $999,999. The Medicare line items will remain the same however the tax deduction for Medicare would be lowered from 1.45% to 1% of earned income but would cover all incomes up to $250,000.

Genius Medical Coverage Benefits

A new line item would be added to the W-2GE to cover Genius healthcare coverage which would now become a payroll deduction for all Genius class employees. In an effort to provide flexibility for employers in providing healthcare coverage to its employees they will have the option of opting out of the employer mandate in the Affordable Care Act. By opting out they would agree to make the minimum wage for employees of these classes $9.00 per hour and agree to match employee contributions for self or family coverage through the Genius healthcare payroll deduction line item. The payroll deduction for all single workers would be 3% of all wages and tips earned on a pretax basis. Married tax payers would be subject to a 6% payroll deduction. All taxpayers would be subject to a 1% payroll deduction for each dependent child that they claim on the Genius W-4 form. All employees who are enrolled in the Genius healthcare program would be mandated to be enrolled in federal healthcare exchanges and would also be removed from their states' Medicaid rolls and the funding for each participant would have to be remitted back to the Department of Health and Human Services to defray the costs of the Affordable Care Act.

$10.13 per hour

This will be the Genius wage for all US citizens and permanent residents in all job classes other than tip wage employees, farm payroll agricultural workers, and penal system employees. Employers may choose to keep employees under current Social Security rules and choose to implement the Affordable Care Act mandates. Employers will again have the option to forego Affordable Care mandates and place employees in Genius class for all workers who work less than 37.5 hours per week. Employees who are less than fulltime employees will have the option at the beginning of their employment or at the time of an employment status change from full time to part time to join the Genius class. That will enable them to forego their employer benefit plans and enroll in a federal exchange healthcare plan within 90 days of the start of their employment or notification of a status. They would have to fill out a new Genius W-4 with their employer to begin Genius class deductions. Fulltime employees working more than 37.5 hours per week will only be able to opt in to Genius healthcare benefits by mutual agreement with their employer. Employers would be responsible for matching employee contributions to the Genius healthcare plans.

$11.13 per hour

This will be the Genius Intern/Training wage for employees pursuing careers covered under the Genius Act including all federal government interns/trainees and contractors. Employers will not be required to provide healthcare benefits for these positions but would still need to provide matching payroll deductions for interns/trainees who opt to use Genius medical coverage during their internship. Workers will only be able to be paid a trainee/intern wage for a maximum of 1,000 hours.

$13.13 per (Genius Society base wage)

All workers who join the Genius Society workers union or any of its affiliate unions will make this as their minimum wage. This wage would include any jobs taken by any new immigrants or guest workers or permanent resident visas issued after December 31, 2013. All corporations who sponsor non US citizens for employment would be required to maintain this wage. If the company does not offer medical benefits the employee would be required to register for Genius medical coverage on the federal exchange.

All American multinational companies would maintain these wages for all of their employees worldwide in order to establish a universal standard of living that will become the new symbol for the American Dream. The Department of Commerce would negotiate and mandate that these wage rates and tax rates become standard with all of our allied training partners through the Genius Act Trade Treaty. These wage rates would also be negotiated with our North American trade partners Canada & Mexico through a Genius addendum to NAFTA. All citizens of these countries would be required to join the Genius Society in order to granted permanent residency status.

By lifting the fortunes of the workers who occupy the lowest classes of all workers and employing the "trickle out" economic theory of employing our prison population we can cure our generational poverty problem and provide them with motivation and ambition to join a Genius Society where hard work, education, and dedication will be rewarded. It will also become the guide for non-American citizens who reach our shores and borders can achieve their version of the American Dream either here or in their own homeland.

The Genius Society (Universal Worker's Union)

In order to truly equalize wages universally and fight the diminishing power of organized labor around the world the *Genius Act* will propose the creation of a new universal organized labor union that will provide clear guide for advancement with rewards for dedication and achievement among workers who join the Society. The Society will fight for the equalization of salary and benefits for all workers who have commensurate experience while also battling inflation and raises in the cost of living by implementing policies that not only include automatic raises in worker's pay for every two to three years of experience but give them the opportunity to purchase a spot in a higher classification by paying a higher set of Society dues. It will reward workers for pursuing educational advancement by providing them with automatic salary escalators for attaining educational goals or for receiving professional certifications necessary for their chosen career path. It will still provide the incentives for dedication to their craft by achieving seniority upgrades but also injecting new lifeblood into the workforce by forcing retirement or allowing workers to achieve "emeritus" status in all classifications after 33 years of service to that classification. All workers who achieve 33 years of service to the Society will be eligible to receive to receive a prorated retirement benefit from their National Retirement Savings account no matter their age with full benefits commencing once they attain the age of 62.5 years of age. They will receive Genius medical benefits deducted from their "emeritus" payments up until they reach the age of 62.5 as well with deductions ceasing once they have attained that age. We will now delve into the details of how the Genius Society will become the standard of worldwide excellence in organized labor.

Joining the Society

All workers of job classes covered by the Genius Act would be eligible to join the Genius Society. Each new member would be responsible for making an initial payment of $1300 to the Debt Society fund in order to purchase their initial classification card. Half of the proceeds of their initial membership fee would go to the US Treasury to maintain Genius programs managed by the federal government. The remaining half would be managed by the Society to cover management and administration costs including creating a new Genius profile and processing of all certifications and educational achievements to determine their job classification status as they enter their profession. Veterans Society dues would be paid from the Department of Veterans Affairs budget. Workers who are faced with financial difficulties in making their initial society Debt payment but are qualified to join a job class will be allowed to have their payment made through payroll deduction in increments of 10% of their salary until their dues are paid in full. All non-citizens including permanent residents and work permit holders will be required to pay their Debt Society dues in advance of them beginning work or have their corporation sponsor their dues with a minimum payment of 50% of their dues to cover administrative costs of creating a Genius ID profile for them. Genius Society dues will increase by $100 every two years for a period of 12 years followed by an increase in the 13th year before dues are reset to their initial base year levels. The maximum initial dues will be $2000 with top classification dues being $3300. Each member will only be able to purchase a classification card 3 levels above the classification that they are provisionally qualified for.

Determining Job Class Classification

Each new member of the Genius Society will have a Genius ID profile created for them. They will each have a job class classification done for them determined based on their experience, education, and certifications necessary to perform their profession. Each profession will have their own standards for determining certification and education necessary to attain automatic placement in specific classes. Employees will be required to provide veritable proof of education and experience in order to receive their classification. Members will receive an advancing letter classification with the lowest class being Q for Qualified with the second lowest class being M and the highest class being A. General Genius classifications will mandate that all holders of associate's degrees automatically receive M classification. Holders of bachelor's degrees will receive L classifications. Holders of Master's or specialist degrees will receive an automatic J classification. Holders of Doctorate degrees will receive an automatic G classification. All honorably discharged veterans of all branches of the military will be given a M classification. Trainees and interns or non-qualified members of a professional class will receive a T classification which will allow them to work a maximum of 1,000 in a calendar year learning that profession. They must then be moved to a qualified classification or be classified as a non-Genius employee. Each employee's classification will be denoted in their Genius ID. For US citizens their classification will be the 3rd digit of their Genius ID, for non US citizens it will be the 7th digit of their Genius ID.

Career Advancement

All qualified members in classifications Q=Qualified through classification H will receive automatic classification increases for every two years of service or 4000 hours worked in that classification. Workers in the G classification will receive their classification increase after 1 year or 2000 hours of service. Workers in classes F through B will receive an automatic increase after 6000 hours or 3 years of service at each level. Workers at B classification or lower will be required to perform 10,000 of service to receive automatic increases to an A classification. All workers who achieve an A classification will be required to retire or be moved to "emeritus" status after 3 years of service in that class. All workers will be required to complete at least of 250 hours of recertification training during their automatic advancement period and pass a recertification exam before receiving their automatic class increase. Workers will have the opportunity to advance up to 3 classifications above their current class by taking a certification exam for that class and paying the difference in Society dues between their aspiring class and their current class. All classes may be advanced into except the A and G classes. International workers or workers converting from other unions will be allowed to purchase the right to enter a classification based upon their experience and education or certifications. Workers will be rewarded with pay increases and pay escalators as they move into higher classifications.

Genius Pay Scale & Education Escalators

The Genius Society will establish a base pay rate for all jobs covered under the Genius Act but each profession will have the discretion to set their own base pay rate for its profession. The Society will recommend that pay raises be distributed evenly over each of the 13 qualified classes with "A" class workers receiving a pay rate that is exactly 100% higher than that of a "Qualified" worker. Workers will have the opportunity to receive pay escalators for achieving certain educational and certification goals. Workers will also receive pay escalators for achieving language and financial literacy proficiencies so that they may become global employees in their profession. Workers in the Genius Society will receive the following pay escalators for their achievements:

10% increase for receiving an Associate's degree with a minimum classification of M class

15% increase for receiving a Bachelor's degree with a minimum classification of L class

20% increase for receiving a Master's/Specialist degree with a minimum classification of J class

25% increase for receiving a Doctorate degree with a minimum classification of G class

They will also receive increases in their pay for achieving the following proficiencies.

5% increase for achieving language proficiency in the following languages (Russian, Spanish, Mandarin, Portuguese, and Afrikaans)

5% increase for achieving proficiency in financial literacy, health care administrator, or Certified Tax Preparer.

Genius Society Benefit Plans

The Genius Society will create an environment that will benefit the greater good of all workers but will create a truly collaborative and cooperative economy between all Society members and the companies that they work for. As discussed before all members will be enrolled in the Genius Medical benefit program that will lower their healthcare costs for themselves and their dependents but receive all the benefits of joining the Society. They will have lower payroll tax deductions for Social Security and Medicare as they will be covered under the newly created Medical & Retirement Savings Act that will lower their Retirement Savings deduction to 4.5% and their Medicare deduction to 1%. They will also be able to set up new National 401(k) plan accounts in which they will have an automatic payroll deduction of 2.5% which would be matched by their employer with additional matching of up to 5% of their gross income through elective deferrals. In addition, the Society will request a 2% royalty on all hours worked by members from all employers so that it may make an additional annual contribution of $1,000 + 1% of each member's salary to their Retirement Savings accounts. The Society will also pledge to make at least 10% of its net profits to charitable endeavors related to its members including employee education assistance and affordable housing for its members. The Society will also implement a matching grant program for employee charitable contributions up to 10% of its net profits.

Genius Society Emeritus Pension Program

All workers who serve 33 years to the Genius Society will become eligible to enter the Emeritus Pension Program. Under this program retiring workers will be eligible to receive a benefit equal to a "Qualified" workers annual salary at the time of them entering the program no matter their age. They can continue to work but will receive wages equal to a M class worker so that we can stimulate the process of advancement of other workers. If they are 62.5 years old they would be eligible to receive a National Retirement account benefit and also be able to access their National 401(k) account without penalty no matter their age. Emeritus Pension benefits will last for a period of 20 years from the last day of employment for each worker and they would receive Genius medical benefits for life.

The following table will be the base wage rate for Genius Society Professional workers.

Genius Society Base Wage Table

Classification Level	Society Dues to Join Classification	Annual Society Dues	Base Wage Rate Per Hour	Years of Service Required	Estimated % of Workforce in Classification
A	$2,600	$260	$26.26	3 years	1%
B	$2,500	$250	$25.25	3 years	5%
C	$2,400	$240	$24.24	3 years	6%
D	$2,300	$230	$23.23	3 years	7%
E	$2,200	$220	$22.22	3 years	8%
F	$2,100	$210	$21.21	3 years	9%
G	$2,000	$200	$20.20	1 year	10%

H	$1,900	$190	$19.19	2 years	7%
I	$1,800	$180	$18.18	2 years	5%
J	$1,700	$170	$17.17	2 years	6%
K	$1,600	$160	$16.16	2 years	7%
L	$1,500	$150	$15.15	2 years	8%
M	$1,400	$140	$14.14	2 years	9%
Qualified	$1,300	$130	$13.13	2 years	10%
Trainee/Intern			$11.13	1,000 hours	

Non-qualified Genius class workers and non-Genius class jobs would be subject to a minimum wage of $10.13 per hour with all workers receiving a cost of living adjustment of at least 1% per year and a maximum of 5% annually based on inflation tied to CPI. Inmate employees, tip employees, and farm payroll workers would be paid a minimum wage of $9.00 per hour which would increase at a fixed rate of 1% per year.

The Genius Society would create a world of equalized wages and revitalize organized labor in America and globally by "raising the level of all ships" while stopping the erosion of jobs due to the tidal wave of outsourcing brought on by a recent era of capitalistic cannibalism. The Genius Act will seek to increase consumers spending power by increasing wages and the number of available jobs while also implementing revolutionary tax reforms that will be discussed in the next chapter that will launch America and the world into a New World of economic prosperity.

IX.   Genius Act Tax Reforms & Genius Tax Rate Schedule

The original concept of the *Genius Act* was to create a series of tax reforms that would widen the base of available taxpayers by creating an environment where employers would hire more workers and pay them at rates that would make all of them "makers" instead of "takers". Employers would be rewarded with lower tax rates and flexibility of income to allow them to invest back into their businesses. The Internal Revenue Service and the Treasury Department would be able to close the tax gap by introducing the revolutionary Certified Tax Preparer Program which I will introduce in the next chapter, and cutting tax expenditures and discretionary spending in the federal budget to reduce or eliminate the deficit and eventually the national debt. Getting more employees back working would also allow the government to cut aid to poverty programs like SNAP and Medicaid and reduce tax expenditures on Earned Income Tax Credit and Additional Child Tax Credit, while reducing their federal tax liability to allow them higher take home pay during the year. This increase in disposable income for lower and middle class workers would spark in an increase in consumption which in turn leads to higher revenues for the Treasury. We will outline several of these controversial tax reforms as well as a proposal for a Genius Tax Rate Schedule which we believe would lead to an American and worldwide economic recovery.

The Genius Act

Tax Reforms

Medical & Retirement Savings Act

The first tax reform proposed through *Genius Act* is a total overhaul of the Social Security & Medicare systems whose federal budget outlays have grown at an unsustainable rate as "baby boomers" have left the workforce and are living longer putting a tremendous strain on America's budgets and deficits. The solution to this problem would be the creation of the Medical & Retirement Savings Act. Under this plan new Genius employees would pay lower taxes through payroll deduction line items but would also receive lower retirement benefits but receive a lifetime of equivalent healthcare benefits as medical care savings are achieved through the Affordable Care Act as benefits providers have to lower costs to compete with federal exchange programs. In exchange for lower retirement benefits through the Social Security program, workers would be eligible to set up National 401(K) accounts or National Retirement Savings Accounts to offset that loss in benefits. Employees will also have the choice on whether they prefer the market driven 401(k) accounts or the defined benefit of Retirement Savings accounts but would also have the security of employer matching and government subsidies for a period of time that have the potential to drastically improve their net worth over time. Here is a comparison of between current systems and Genius Act reforms:

Social Security vs. Retirement Savings Act

Under the current Social Security payroll deduction worker's pay 6.21% of their income up to $118,000 to cover their defined benefit contribution for Social Security. Under the Retirement Savings Act workers contribution would be reduced to 4.5% on incomes up to $250,000 and 2.5% on incomes between $250,001 and $999,999 with payroll deduction phasing out at incomes above $1 Million annually. Lower wage earners (those with 20 quarters of earnings with an average annual income of less than $119,000) will see a reduction in Social Security benefits by 50% if they work at least 20 quarters under the Genius system. High wage earners (those earning an average of $119,000 or more annual over 20 quarters) will face a reduction of 25% of their Social Security benefits.

Employees will be able to offset this loss of benefits by taking advantage of a Retirement Savings contribution credit direct from the US Treasury to their retirement accounts after they have filed their annual tax returns. Employees will be able to receive matching of up to 9% of their income up to $9,999 and receive a dollar for dollar tax credit from the Treasury and their employer with the employer and the Treasury equally responsible for the matching for a period of 5 years. Here is a table of how employee's benefits would change as they work more quarters under the Retirement Savings Account system:

The Genius Act

Benefit	Social Security		National Retirement Savings	
Quarters worked in Genius System	Benefit % for employee w/ Government & Employer Match	Benefit % with employer match only	Benefit % for employee w/ Government & Employer Match	Benefit % for employee with employer match only
0-4	100	93	0	7
4-8	86	89	14	11
8-12	71	80	29	20
12-16	63	69	37	31
16-20	57	60	43	40
20+	50	57	50	43

Federal obligations for Social Security benefits will be reduced as workers are employed more quarters under the Genius system. This will allow workers who remain on the Social Security system to lower the eligibility age to 62.5 years for all workers by 2030 and allow it to remain solvent in perpetuity. Workers would then be able to set up their own tax deferred accounts through the National Retirement Savings Program managed by the Thrift Savings Program (TSP).

Genius Medical benefits vs. Medicare

Under the Genius system workers would also face lower tax payments for Medicare payroll deductions as opposed to the current system. For non-Genius Society employees the payroll deduction would be 1% of earned income as opposed to the current deduction which is 1.45%. Genius class employees would be responsible for deduction on incomes up to $250,000 as opposed to the current income limit of $119,000. Workers who are members of the Genius Society would not be required to make a payroll deduction payment as they will be eligible for Genius medical benefits if they are employed by the Society for 33 years. All employees would become eligible for Medicare benefits at the age of 62.5 starting in 2030.

The Genius Medical Benefit contribution would be introduced as a line item on all Genius class employees. This will require a payroll deduction for all workers starting at 3% for single taxpayers or 6% on married taxpayers claiming their spouses as a dependent on their W-4. Taxpayers would also make an additional contribution of 1% of their income for any dependent children under the age of 26 that they intend to claim on their tax return. Employers would then be mandated to match contributions made by employees and would receive tax credit equal to 10% of any amounts paid for employee benefit plans.

Tax Expenditures & Itemized Deductions

The Genius Act

In order to promote compromise between employers, employees, and Congressional leaders concerned about budgetary restraints the Genius Act will propose a series of tax reforms that will allow employees and corporations to receive lower tax rates while receiving higher wages. Congress will maintain budget discipline by limiting deductions and reducing tax expenditures.

Here are the proposed changes to tax expenditures that *Genius Act* would recommend:

Standard Deduction

Filing Status	Current	Genius Recommendations
Single	$5,950	$5,000
Married Filing Jointly	$11,900	$10,500
Married Filing Separately	$5,950	$5,000
Head of Household	$8,700	$7,500
Qualifying Widow(er)	11,900	$10,500

Personal Exemptions

The current personal exemption amount for each person claimed on a tax return is **$3,800** with phase out limitations based on income limits for each filing status. The Genius Act will propose the following simplified changes to exemption amounts and phase out limits

Exemption Amount	Income limit (per household)
$3,000	Up to $250,000
$2,000	$250,001-$400,000
$1,500	$400,001-$999,999
$0	$1,000,000

Itemized Deductions

The *Genius Act* will also propose changes to itemized deductions to offset the changes in tax rates that would result from implementation of Genius tax rates. Here is a list of itemized deductions and their limitations under the Genius Act for taxpayers making $400,000 or less.

Deduction	Genius Limitation
Interest Paid	$50,000
Charitable Contributions	$50,000
Medical Deductions	All expenses above 5% of income
Taxes Paid	$25,000
Miscellaneous Deductions	$5,000 or over 1% of income with documentation

There would also be a reduction in the charitable and business mileage rates used to calculate deductions. Medical and charitable miles would be reduced to $.18/mile and business miles to $.435/mile.

Genius taxpayers who have annual incomes above $400,000 will have their itemized deductions limited to 33% of their total income.

Adjustments to Income

Teachers would be allowed to receive an adjustment of up to $1,000 for supplies purchased for their classrooms or school districts.

Students repaying student loans will now have the opportunity to deduct student loan interest paid with adjusted gross incomes up to $150,000 for single taxpayers or $400,000 for married filing joint taxpayers.

Tax Credits

The Genius Act will make some controversial changes to some of the most popular tax credits but changes will be needed to improve quality of life of all taxpayers and reduce tax burdens for all to lift taxpayers out of poverty. The two programs that will face the most changes are the refundable credits of Earned Income Credit and the Additional Child Tax Credit. The Genius Act will however, introduce a Financial Literacy Credit to offset some of losses of wealth that taxpayers experienced during the "Great Recession" as well as a expansion of the American Opportunity educational credit explained earlier to reward those who pay down their educational debt.

Financial Literacy Credit

As explained earlier in Genius Act, taxpayers who complete a financial literacy course and proficiency exam will be eligible to receive a $1,000 tax credit under the American Opportunity Education Act of 2013. These taxpayers will also be eligible to receive a refundable credit of 10% of any 1099-A or 1099-C debt that they have had forgiven since 2008 up to a credit maximum of $5,000. They would need to receive a revised 1099 from the financial institution showing a 10% reduction in the original forgiveness. The financial institution would also receive a tax credit equal to 1% of the total amount that they have forgiven since the start of the financial crisis. Financial institutions would also be able to revise their corporate tax returns to claim a 10% reduction in their interest income from 2010, 2011, and 2012. This will become a Genius addendum to the Dodd Frank Act. In return, tax payers and financial institutions would agree to a 1% financial transaction tax on any sales of assets over $99,999. This tax will go to the FDIC reserve fund to cover any claims.

The Genius Act

Education Credits

Under provisions of the Genius Education Act detailed earlier students and graduates will be able to receive education credits up to $5,000 later increasing to $7,500 to cover amounts paid for education and the repayment of student loan debt. They will be able to deduct education expenses up to $2,500 as a dollar for dollar credit or 25% of their costs with a credit maximum of $5,000. They will also be able to deduct 10% of their principal payments made on their student loans up to a credit maximum of $5,000. The credit will expand over the next 5 years to a maximum of $7,500.

Child Tax Credit and Additional Child Tax Credit

Under the Genius Act the Child Tax Credit and the Refundable Additional Child Tax Credit would experience a reduction of 10% of the overall credit value. It will however achieve an expansion of the number of households that qualify for the credit as the income limitations will be expanded to include household incomes up to $999,999. These are the proposed Genius Act changes to the credit.

Credit Amount	Income Threshold (per household)
$900	Up to $100,000
$800	$100,001-$400,000
$600	$400,001-$999,999
$0	$1,000,000+

Earned Income Tax Credit (EITC)

The Genius Act would propose drastic changes to the Earned Income Tax Credit program, one of the most successful anti-poverty programs in American history. The Genius Act would propose a 10% cut to the program and also propose lower income limits on when the credit would phase out to encourage employers to pay higher wages to lower class employees throughout the year. By lowering overall tax rates and encouraging employers to pay wages that will allow their employees to move into the middle class we can end the scourge of poverty and dependency that the crutch of the Earned Income Credit had provided for nearly the last 3 decades. Here are the proposed income limits for single and married taxpayers claiming the credit.

Number of Qualifying Children	Single/Head of Household	Married Filing Jointly
0	$9,999	$13,333
1	$27,599	$33,133
2	$31,099	$36,339

3	$33,933	$39,933

Genius Tax Rate Schedule

Above any other principle discussed in the *Genius Act* the overriding goal was to take great strides in simplifying the tax code and lowering tax rates for all taxpayers and corporations. While creating jobs and new streams of revenue for the Treasury became a larger part of this journey the changes to the tax code and the tax rate schedule remain the integral part of what makes the Genius Act work. By broadening the tax base by increasing the number of "makers" in the economy we can decrease the burden of all taxpayers no matter their income level. Lowering taxes will "raise the level of all ships" from the dinghies to the super yachts and all vessels in between and the Genius Tax Rate Schedule will bring a tidal wave of economic prosperity. We will discuss the changes to the corporate tax rates later; we will now delve into the individual tax rates for Genius class taxpayers. Tax rates will remain progressive in that those that make the most will be expected to pay more in taxes, but the tax brackets will be flatter for easier tracking of tax liability and planning for obligations. It will also spur job growth as employers will now be able to plan their obligations before making hiring decisions or deciding to expand their business into new territories as they will have lower federal tax burdens in considering their corporate domiciling options.

All Genius class taxpayers will report their income on a newly created 1040 GE that will contain all of the tax code changes that pertain to their tax status. Unlike standard 1040 forms the tax rates will be the same for all filing statuses as the tax rates will be based on each household. All credits and their eligibility requirements will remain the same as well as exemption eligibility rules.

Genius Individual Tax Rates

Earned (Wage) Income

Taxable Income per Household	Tax Rate on Income
$0-$9,999	0 tax liability
$10,000-$99,999	9% tax liability
$100,000-$399,999	18% tax liability
$400,000-$999,999	27% tax liability
$1,000,000+	33% tax liability

All tax rates would be progressive so taxpayers would pay zero federal income tax on the first $9,999 of their income, 9% on income between $10,000 and $99,999 and continuing until they

The Genius Act

reach the top bracket of 33% on income above $1,000,000. All tax brackets will be progressive in a similar fashion.

Short Term Capital Gains (including real estate held less than 1 year)

Capital Gain per household	Tax Rate on Capital Gain
0-$99,999	9% tax liability
$100,000-$399,999	18% tax liability
$400,000-$999,999	27% tax liability
$1,000,000+	33% tax liability

* Unlike current tax policy Short Term and Long Term Capital Gains Taxes will be independent of taxpayers Earned income in determining their tax liability.

Long Term Capital Gains including Primary Home Real Estate Sales Gains

Capital Gain Per Household	Tax Rate on Capital Gain
0-$9,999	0 tax liability
$10,000-$99,999	9% tax liability
$100,000-$399,999	18% tax liability
$400,000-$10,000,000	27% tax liability
$10,000,000+	33% tax liability

*All Capital Gains Transactions with a net gain of $99,999 or more will be subject to a Financial Transactions tax of 1% to be remitted to the newly created Society Debt Fund to reduce America's Debt obligations.

Rent, Royalty, and Intellectual Property Income (including S-corps)

Rent, Royalty Income Per Household	Tax Rate on Royalty Income
0-$99,999	9% tax liability
$100,000-$399,999	18% tax liability
$400,000-$10,000,000	27% tax liability
$10,000,000+	33% tax liability

Farm Income (sole proprietor and S-Corp farms)

Farm Income Per Household	Tax Rate on Farm Income
0-$99,999	9% tax liability
$100,000-$399,999	18% tax liability
$400,000-$1,999,999	27% tax liability
$2,000,000+	33% tax liability

*Farms that employ agricultural workers other than family members will be subject to Genius Corporate Farm income tax rates based on the number of workers they employ at Genius Tax Rates.

All other income and Retirement Plan withdrawals

Other/Retirement Income Per Household	Tax Rate on Other/Retirement Income
0-$9,999	0 tax liability
$10,000-$99,999	9% tax liability
$100,000-$399,999	18% tax liability
$400,000+	27% tax liability

Genius Corporate Tax Rate Schedule

The Genius Individual tax rates were based around creating equality among all taxpayers by lowering the tax rates for all working class Americans while rewarding successful taxpayers by lowering top tax rates to promote the "trickle out" economy. The Genius Corporate tax rates will focus on job creation by making lower tax rates available to the employers who employ the most Genius class employees. Employers will be allowed to apply for Genius class designation and receive these tax rates based on the number of Genius employees on their payroll who work at least 1,000 hours during that company's fiscal year. These rates will also apply to government and non-profit entities that create new for profit entities only to employ Genius rate employees. Here is a chart of tax brackets on net operating incomes based on the number of qualified Genius class employees.

Net Operating Income Tax Rates

	Tax Rate Thresholds			
Number of Genius Class Employees	9%	18%	27%	33%
1-100	0-$99,999	$100,000-$499,999	$500,000-$1,500,000	$1,500,000+
101-500	0-$250,000	$250,001-$999,999	$1,000,000-$2,999,999	$3,000,000+
501-1000	0-$999,999	$1,000,000-$5,000,000	$5,000,000-$10,000,000	$10,000,000+
1001+	0-$4.99 million	$5 million-$15 million	$15 million-$49.99 million	$50 million+

Corporate Passive Activity Real Estate, Rent, Royalty, Intellectual Property Income

The Genius Act

Number of Genius Class Employees	Tax Rate Thresholds			
	9%	18%	27%	33%
1-100	0-$250,000	$250,000-$1 million	$1 million-$5 million	$5,000,000+
101-500	0-$1 million	$1.01 million-$4.99 million	$5 million-$14.99 million	$15,000,000+
501-1000	0-$2.5 million	$2.51 million-$10 million	$10 million-$25 million	$25 million+
1001+	0-$4.99 million	$5 million-$15 million	$15 million-$49.99 million	$50 million+

Short Term Capital Gain Tax Rates

Number of Genius Class Employees	Tax Rate Thresholds			
	9%	18%	27%	33%
1-100	0-$500,000	$500,001-$1.5 million	$1.5 million-$5 million	$5 million+
101-500	0-$1.5 million	$1.5 million-$5 million	$5 million-$15 million	$15 million+
501-1000	0-$3 million	$3 million-$15 million	$15 million-$33 million	$33 million+
1001+	0-$4.99 million	$5 million-$24.99 million	$25 million-$49.99 million	$50 million+

*All stock or asset sales of more than $99,999 will result in a 1% Capital Transaction Tax that will paid to the Society Debt Fund to cover Debt Servicing.

Long Term Capital Gains Tax Rate

Number of Genius Class Employees	9%	18%	27%	33%
1-100	0-$500,000	$500,001-$1.5 million	$1.5 million-$5 million	$5 million+
101-500	0-$2.5 million	$2.5 million-$5 million	$5 million-$17.49 million	$17.5 million+
501-1000	0-$3 million	$3 million-$15 million	$15 million-$33 million	$33 million+
1001+	0-$4.99 million	$5 million-$33 million	$33 million-$65.99 million	$66 million+

The Genius Act

Agriculture & Farm Income (Genius Class Farm Employers)

	9%	18%	27%	33%
1-100	0-$500,000	$500,001-$1.5 million	$1.5 million-$5 million	$5 million+
101-500	0-$1.5 million	$1.5 million-$5 million	$5 million-$15 million	$15 million+
501-1000	0-$3 million	$3 million-$15 million	$15 million-$33 million	$33 million+
1001+	0-$4.99 million	$5 million-$24.99 million	$25 million-$49.99 million	$50 million+

*These rates will apply for all corporations working on Master Food & Energy Projects and Agricultural & Alternative Energy Suppliers.

Multinational Corporations will be subject to new foreign income tax rates that will allow them to make 1 transfer of up to $1 billion with a transaction tax of 9% per year for the next 5 years. They may make other transfers throughout the year but they would be subject to individual transaction taxes based on the number of Genius class employees working for their company. They may make up 333 transactions in a year. Here are the transaction fees on profits that multinational corporations repatriate into the American economy through American financial institutions.

Foreign Funds Repatriation Tax per Transaction

Number of Genius Class Employees	9%	18%	27%	33%
1-499	0-$1 million	$1 million-$10 million	$10 million-$25 million	$25 million+
500-999	0-$5 million	$5 million-$25 million	$25 million-$75 million	$75million+
1,000-4,999	0-$10 million	$10 million-$50 million	$50 million-$150 million	$150 million+
5,000-9,999	0-$25 million	$25 million-$125 million	$125 million-$500 million	$500 million+
10,000+	0-$50 million	$50 million-$250 million	$250 million-$1 billion	$1 billion+

All foreign asset or stock sales will be subject to a 1% Capital Transactions tax which will be deposited in the Treasury's Debt Society Fund.

Interest Income for Financial Institutions Lending to Genius Employers

The Genius Act

Interest Income per Financial Institution	Interest Income Tax Rate
0-$10 million	9% tax liability
$10 million- $50 million	18% tax liability
$50 million+	27% tax liability

Dividend Income from Genius Class Corporations

Dividend Income Individual		Dividend Income Corporate	
Income Received	Tax Rate	Income Received	Tax Rate
0-$250,000	9% tax liability	0-$10 million	9% tax liability
$250,000-$1 million	18% tax liability	$10 million- $50 million	18% tax liability
$1 million+	27% tax liability	$50 million+	27% tax liability

Corporations will be able to deduct amortization costs up to a maximum of $5,000,000 in their first year of operation as a Genius class employer.

Corporate Energy Saving Transportation Credit

Corporations will be able to deduct the cost of energy saving equipment and alternative energy sources including cars and energy saving transportation and hauling vehicles up to $5 million per year for the next 5 years. There will also be credits for purchasing High Occupancy Vehicles with alternative fuel sources. The credit will be a maximum of $3,000 for individuals on one vehicle per year. For corporations the credit would amount to 10% of the vehicles purchase price or a maximum of $5,000 per vehicle up to a maximum of $1 million per corporation. For cities or municipalities they would be eligible for a credit of up to $25,000 per vehicle to a maximum of $25 million per municipality.

Extension of the HIRE Credit for non-Genius Employers

In an effort to boost payrolls across America, the *Genius Act* will propose an addendum to the HIRE Act that would allow traditional employers not covered under the Genius Act to receive a credit for 20% of the payroll taxes that they paid on all new employees that result in a net gain of jobs added to their payroll for the next 5 years. This Genius addendum to the HIRE Act would also propose the creation of a cabinet level position to be called the Jobs Czar. This position would be occupied by Mitt Romney or another high ranking member of the Republican Party's business elite. There would also be an additional appointment to the post of Assistant Secretary of the Treasury to monitor Genius Act job creation and tax revenue generation to ensure that the program reaches Congressional recommendations in each category. Each appointment would last for a period of 5 years and could be renewed by majority vote of the full Senate. The extensions would be open for federal government agencies to hire new workers responsible for monitoring and collecting taxes from Genius business activity. In the next chapter we will discuss IRS Reforms & Certified Tax/Health Care Consultant Programs.

www.ingramcontent.com/pod-product-compliance
Lightning Source LLC
Chambersburg PA
CBHW021900170526
45157CB00005B/1900